THE SHAPING OF SCOTLAND

THE SHAPING OF SCOTLAND

R J BRIEN

ABERDEEN UNIVERSITY PRESS

First published 1989
Aberdeen University Press
A member of the Maxwell Pergamon Macmillan Group

© R J Brien 1989

British Library Cataloguing in Publication Data
Brien, R. J.
The shaping of Scotland: 18th century patterns of land use and settlement.
1. Scotland. Rural regions. Settlement, history
I. Title
941.1'009734
ISBN 0 08 036572 8

PRINTED IN GREAT BRITAIN
THE UNIVERSITY PRESS
ABERDEEN

CONTENTS

ILLUSTRATIONS

PREFACE

As one who was born in the country and has lived all his life in it I have always been very much in tune with the Scottish landscape and the ways of its people. The countryside being as durable as it is I have never been very far away from history as expressed in rural artifacts. But this sense started both to crystallise and to broaden when some twenty years ago, I had access to Panton's map of Craigyloch (shown in Figure 1), an area I knew well. It became very clear to me then that the landscape itself, both in the agricultural and the social sense, was profoundly different two hundred years ago. But how had it changed?

This question became a constant preoccupation for me and led to the research which lies behind this book. In carrying out these searches, all in the works of eighteenth-century writers, I became aware how profound the changes have been and how quickly they came about (in relative terms). I also became aware how little the ordinary man knows about these changes—most people seem to assume that Scotland has always been more or less as it is today.

Practically nothing remains today to give the least idea of the landscape or the extremely primitive rural life in Scotland two centuries ago. Most of the buildings that can still be seen belonged to people of some wealth, not to ordinary men far less to those who were forced to seek a living in another country. Thus visitors from overseas coming home to the land of their forefathers might find it hard to believe how different was the land that their great-great-grandfathers left compared with the fields and woods of today.

This book, then, focuses very broadly on the eighteenth century as a time when profound changes took place which ultimately produced the country we now know. Its aim is to paint a realistic picture of the rural landscape then, how people lived in it and how both people and landscape changed. This is a difficult task for both original conditions and change varied widely in space and time, making generalisations hazardous. Furthermore there is considerable emphasis on the Angus and Perthshire regions, with which I am most familiar. Nevertheless, warts and all, that is the objective of this book.

I recorded for many years the old facts, written by people who had seen and examined the countryside at first hand, in the eighteenth-century, that I have now written in this book. I was content to have collected them and to give them to someone else to prepare a book. As I was preparing to visit an old friend, Professor James Wilson, in Vancouver, Canada, he suggested I bring my notes with me. Hoping he would be willing to write the book, I happily complied, only to find that Jim and his wife felt strongly that I must finish the task I had started, and do the writing myself. So despite my misgivings I started then and there. In the following year Jim came over to Perthshire and completed the book by editing my draft.

My grateful thanks go to Jim, and to the friends who encouraged me to have this book printed, believing that this account, of the Shaping of Scotland would be of interest to many others. And that is my hope.

R J BRIEN
Pitcairngreen
Perthshire
Scotland

INTRODUCTION

Bob Brien is one of the small band of people who, after retirement, maintain a sharp intellectual interest and build on it. He has been retired for twenty-four years, and has made such profitable use of his time that the present volume on *The Shaping of Scotland* has resulted. He claims that his interests are limited to land use, and to the period before 1800, and indeed much of the book is concerned with that subject and time, but nevertheless it has important implications for later periods also.

The book, as he comments himself, has a considerable emphasis on Angus and Perthshire. This is appropriate in more ways than one, but particularly in view of Bob Brien's own background. He can trace his roots back in the area for several generations, to 1725. He went to Cortachy School, at a time when his grandfather was Master of Works on the Airlie Estates at Cortachy. He himself served an apprenticeship with the Glamis Estate, and was in charge of the buildings there. He therefore has an almost inbred knowledge of estate workings and management, and estates are basic to the history of land use in Scotland. For the ten years before he retired, he was the water and drainage engineer for Perthshire, and became thoroughly familiar with what lay under the ground as well as with its surface. It is on this broad basis of long personal experience, allied to wide reading of books and manuscripts, that his book has been written.

The period about which he writes, the eigtheenth century, is a most important one for Scotland. It was then that the patterns of land use and settlement that we now know began to be shaped, in an all-embracing agricultural improvement movement that made rural Scotland for a time one of the fastest changing places in Europe. It is the period when new villages with domestic-industrial emphases began to be shaped, and when water-powered industry was starting to bring to estate owners fresh capital that could be put into improvement. There was widespread surveying of estates, and capitalistic rather than subsistence views of estate management were making themselves felt. The demographic consequences were immense, though that is a story for others to tell. Bob Brien concentrates on the technical background and in so doing, helps to lay a basis of understanding against which the human situation can be judged.

The book contains a great deal of interesting material and much thought. It is an achievement that will bring pleasure and instruction to many, and it is a matter of gratification for me to have been associated with it in some small way.

ALEXANDER FENTON
Director
European Ethnological
Research Centre
Edinburgh

1 A GLIMPSE OF THE RUN-RIGS

The shaping of a nation's landscape is normally a slow and
sporadic process triggered from time to time by a variety of
forces. In this sense Scotland's experience is no exception.
However in her case there was one relatively short period
following the 1715 and 1745 rebellions when the pace of change
accelerated astoundingly, eventuating in the rural landscape we
know today. That period and that change are the subject of this
book.

The Scottish scene in that period—roughly the middle and
latter half of the eighteenth century—was still dominated by the
'run-rig' system of agriculture, a system in which social,
institutional and technological factors were completely
intertwined. There are few records of this scene. However one
unique map, now lodged in West Register House in Edinburgh,
describes in detail the pattern of some 100 acres in Angus as they
were under the run-rig system. This map, 'Craigyloch in the
Parish of Lintrathen' (Figure 1) was drawn by Montrose land
surveyor William Panton for a purpose particularly appropriate
to this book—to facilitate the breaking up and enclosure of the
area as it was then and the transfer of parts to larger adjacent
farms. It shows in carefully measured detail not only the main
types of land we will be discussing and a number of key features
of the settlement (houses, yards, tofts, wells, trees, and a kiln) but
the individual parcels of land and the names of the people who
worked them. This is the only one of about forty of Panton's maps
in Register House to show such detail. The surveyors of that age
were not so much concerned with the existing land structure as
with the new enclosure pattern they were employed to map out.

The subject of this map is a 'ferm toun'—the houses and land
of a group of people who cultivated communally the area, using
a plough team to draw the old Scots plough. The central feature

2   The form of the run-rigs

of the land at that date was the 'inbye' (infield) land, the
irregular masses of long, narrow, curving strips of land—the run-
rigs produced by the method of cultivation bearing that name.
These masses, covering the arable parts of the area, are
surrounded by the 'outbye' (outfield) lands, those unsuitable (at
that time) for continuous cultivation, whether by reason of poor
soil, steep slopes or lack of drainage, and used by the local
population for grazing, pasturing or cutting turf. This ferm toun
was about $\frac{1}{2}$ mile long and $\frac{1}{4}$ mile deep and was traversed by a
road leading to a ford across the River Isla near Airlie Castle in
the County of Angus, now Tayside region.

The rigs themselves were long, sinuous mounds of piled-up soil
separated by hollows or 'baulks' of bare wasteland from which
the soil had been pared by years of scraping and thrown by the
action of the plough towards the centre of the rig (Figure 2).
According to writers of these times the landscape so produced
was 'like a piece of striped cloth' and 'ridged like the waves of the
sea'. In the Craigyloch case the holdings vary from 200 to 400
yards long and from 10 to 25 yards wide. There were no fences,
the baulks separated the rigs and the holdings of one man from
another's.

These holdings were worked by thirteen families whose tracts
were scattered throughout the area, no farmer holding two
adjacent strips. The families lived in small irregular clusters of
houses, each house being adjoined by a yard and a 'toft' or hand-
dug area, the former surrounded by a stone-and-turf wall. In
addition to the farmers' families about thirty others, labourers
with no claim to land also lived in the ferm toun.

In many ways this scene was a microcosm of rural Scotland at
that time—a small island of cultivated land in a sea of rough,
bare, untamed country. In it some thirty families strove without
respite to wrest a meagre and tenuous living from the land, which
was the source of everything they had—food, clothing and

housing. It illustrates some of the main features of the rural landscape—the ferm toun, the division of land, and the run-rigs typical of the inbye area. One significant element is missing— summer shielings, the upland grazing areas to which the women and children of the toun would drive the cattle and stay there with them during the summer months. This introduces the Scottish rural scene as it was in the middle of the eighteenth century. It is now time to elaborate that scene and the changes that were taking place and the forces behind them—the advent of the metal plough, of drainage, of liming of the soil, and probably most of all the realisation by people of substance and enterprise that, given appropriate organisation and management, land could be made more productive and financially profitable.

2 THE BACKGROUND OF CHANGE

By the early part of the eighteenth century Scotland had evolved
a very distinctive social and land tenure system. Huge areas of
land had been gifted from time to time by the monarch of the day
to a favoured few. Under these landowners or lairds the limited
areas that were cultivated were occupied largely by 'possessors',
'kindly tenants' who held their land at the whim of the Laird,
who was himself subject in turn to the whim of the monarch. The
ties that bound laird and possessors together were ties of common
safety and well being, for these were lawless times in which
families, clans and districts warred against one another, and the
lands were subject to constant plunder. 'Prior to 1733 the lord
lived in his castle or tower of war'; 'He was safe there at night and
reasonably safe, unless surprised, outside the castle in the day
time.'(30) The possessors—who would also shelter in the castle
in time of stress—not only lived near each other in ferm touns but
shared the cultivated land communally in the run-rig system of
agriculture. 'All the farmers and vassals resisted commonly the
plunderer since everyone had a share at risk. This was the bond
that made run-rig so necessary in many areas of Scotland up to
1733.'(19)

This communalistic society was not legalistic or feudal. The
aristocratic families held the power and the vassals the property.
The vassals served the Laird in war, worked the land and paid
rent in kind. The system was supported however by an
appropriate complex of customs and institutions which
governed its working relationships. For example cattle, the
source and status symbol of wealth in the lowlands and
southfacing glens, and literally the life blood of the nation, were
all intermixed so that it was in everyone's interest to arm and
resist robbers. Furthermore in the run-rig system the strips of the
inbye land worked by individual families were often intermixed

4

with others' strips (as was the case in Craigyloch—see Figure 1),
again forming a common mass in which everyone had a stake.
The outbye land of which little is shown on this particular map
was largely possessed in common for pasture, occasional
cultivation and the cutting of 'feal' or divots, the source of fuel
and house-building material.

As to property, not only the land but the possessor's house
walls belonged to the Laird since they were derived from his
stones and turf. The roof timbers however were the personal
property of the possessor, for he had cut down the trees which,
like the bogs, 'belonged' to the people and were there for the
taking.If he moved to another place he would take these timbers
with him along with his meagre personal belongings. The
livestock however could belong to the Laird, and in any case
their progeny were likely to return to him as rent.

An important aspect of the culture had to do with succession.
In the early days 'all sons were equal and could farm and were
equal on the clan ground'.(19) Further many of the 'tacksmen'
or prime tenants were related to the Laird by blood rather than
by legal or commercial obligation. This custom, like many
others, was to change—sometimes with drastic consequences for
those affected—when the agricultural revolution took place.

In this early culture the ferm toun and the run-rig style of
cultivation were complementary and key elements. The
dwellings in the ferm toun were 'close together for defence
against the caterans from the North'.(18) Furthermore since no
man alone could operate the massive plough of that day or
support enough horses or oxen to pull it, the ferm touns were also
co-operative working units for cultivation purposes.

Apart from agriculture, Scotland as a whole was already
changing. The independent burghs had been established,
mainly on crossing routes and coastal areas and at estuary
harbours, and men had set up in many trades and crafts—for
example as cattle dealers, fishermen, maltsters, clothiers,
skinners, weavers, wrights and tailors. Such men were without
land or estates and some, though independent of kingly
patronage, became wealthy by employing others. With the
changing times exports to the relatively wealthy south became
possible; overseas and inter-burgh trade sprang up; and
travelling gangs of masons and artificers moved up from the

south to build and embellish the lairds' castles and fortalices as
well as the early bridges. To pay for these improvements cattle
from the glens were traded to southern and eastern parts, many
being driven—on foot—as far as Norfolk, there to be fattened for
the London market. The Reformation and the accompanying
civil war were long past, having witnessed, among other things,
the dissolution of the monasteries with their extensive and often
very progressive Grange lands—which were acquired by the
stronger of the landowners. They had also, of course, left the
country bitterly divided as well as leaving many families,
especially in the interfaces between Highlands and Lowlands, in
a state of divided or shifting loyalty.

Agriculture was not untouched by the general changes in the
country. Land suitable for cultivation was becoming scarce; new
ideas were seeping in regarding ownership of land and
appropriate relationships between landlord and tenant; and
possibly the idea of profit—in money—from land was becoming
more pervasive.

To the middle of the eighteenth century a gradual but
important change in the style of land possession was taking place.
'The earlier divisions of land called "tacks", usually the privilege
of male family relatives, were gradually being converted into
feus and the old possessors became portioners.' (14) This opening
up of land-holding was beneficial to some of the common people,
especially since the run-rig areas on better land, which at an
earlier time were usually worked communally, were now being
divided into farms which a tenant could work with his children
and servants without sub-letting. Thus a tenant who could never
previously have become a tacksman could in time stock one of
these small farms and become independent, not only becoming
less obliged to provide seasonal services to the Laird but being
free to work his land by himself or through sub-tenants. Also the
more energetic of them would rent other fields to expand their
holdings. One of the groups which suffered from these new
arrangements was, of course, the farmers' younger sons;
primogeniture—a concept alien to the earlier Scots culture—
became the rule. 'Now the eldest son fell heir to his fathers
property or stocking, but the younger sons, although bred as
farmers must now work as servants at home or around for want
of stocking.' (19)

Not only were feus or leases coming into use but the conditions they contained were changing. For example the right to cultivate an area was being bound up with obligations, under penalty, to drain, to break in, and to enclose with hedge or wall. Later the Laird in turn undertook to provide the necessary buildings and the house of the farmer, who by the end of the century was moving up in the world and could afford to satisfy his labour needs by employing an ever-growing number of less fortunate men who had lately been possessors.

These substantial changes in the management of large estates had administrative consequences. For example the huge Breadalbane estates in Perthshire, then covering many square miles of mountain and valley, were divided into 'officiaries' or districts, whose ground officers personally presided over the deployment of three, four or five hundred men. These officers were responsible for superintending the working of the vast estate where rent for the farms was levied largely in kind or in services, and they organised this free labour to cut peat in the bogs, cultivate and harvest the home farms, provide and kill the butcher meat for the Laird's household and provide all his transport needs. This sometimes worked to the detriment of both the land and the people, for in later years these landowners' agents or 'factors' were often men from outside the clan, of an alien upbringing—perhaps an English tutor or a 'stickit' lawyer— and inexperienced in land matters, who would come in between the Laird and his people.

In summary, by 1790 the communal ferm toun had disappeared; the old possessor status had gone; leases and feus were now established; and legal paper had displaced the trusted word of the chief.

These evolutionary changes were given a huge impetus by the 1715 and 1745 rebellions, especially the latter. With the failure of the Stuart cause came military roads and English garrisons; the countryside was ravaged; Jacobite lairds were exiled and their families deprived of authority; the lands of the rebel clans were forfeited; and the whole character of the Highlander and the people of the eastfacing glens and lowlands was changed beyond recognition. But these were only the immediate consequences of military victory; what was infinitely more important for the land of Scotland was the work of 'the improvers'.

The government in London established three bodies whose
work and example changed the face of Scotland almost within a
generation—the Commissioners of the Forfeited Estates, the
Trustees for Fisheries, Manufactures and Improvements, and
the Board of Agriculture led by the assiduous Lord Kames of
Blair Drummond. The mandate of the Commissioners was 'to
civilise the inhabitants of these annexed estates and to promote
the Protestant religion, good Government, industry and manufacturers and the principles of loyalty and no other purpose
whatsoever'.(11) Most of the task of improving the state of
agriculture fell to Lord Kames' Commissioners. This body
functioned until 1784, long enough to see the demise of the
generation that had fought at Culloden and long enough to
indoctrinate a new generation of landowners with new ideas.
During this period of 38 years the Commissioners ruled supreme
over most of Scotland until they became redundant when the
forfeited estates were restored to their original heirs. With a free
hand to do as they liked with other people's property—and with
the opportunities which the forfeited estates afforded to
experiment with new ideas—they ruthlessly initiated the
agricultural revolution, which was soon in full swing. Trade and
manufacturing were also expanding, and the stream of rural
people displaced from the land provided ample, cheap labour for
the new industries in the towns.

Measured by the agricultural production of the countryside
and the quality of life in it the efforts of the Commissioners were
undoubtedly successful. Potatoes and turnips were introduced
and much more grain produced; cattle found better food and a
better market at the end of a shorter life; and the black-faced
sheep swept across the landscape. The old whisky stills were
eliminated, the country undoubtedly sobered up, and the much
smaller numbers of people now farming the much larger new
farms were far better off than their predecessors.

The landscape too began to undergo substantial change. The
open, unfenced run-rig land and the free summer pasture on the
mountains started to disappear along with the long,
communally ploughed rigs of grain and the accompanying small
plots of flax; enclosed rectangular fields along with walls, ditches,
fences and tree plantations made their appearance and soon
became universal; in fact the whole appearance of the rural

landscape underwent such a tremendous change that it is extremely difficult today to envisage what the country was like prior to 1750.

The upshot was that a great many people disappeared entirely from the rural scene as the surviving landowners and some from across the southern border began to squeeze the countryside of men and their small holdings. Far fewer people were needed to work the land with the new methods of agriculture and land management. The small farmers lost, without recompense, their age-old right of free grazing on the moors and hillsides; tree-felling on more distant hills was curtailed; even the bogs could only be cut for peat fires with the consent of an ever-smaller number of Heritors. The new small farmer, usually the strongest member of the original communal group of possessors, ousted the cottager with his toft and his cow—the pendicler, the cottar and the run-rig cultivator had to go. In this long act of attrition thousands fled and many died; the most robust took to the colonies, the weaker to the mills and slums of Glasgow and Dundee. This slow, agonising exodus, little known and largely unremarked, was in fact the first of the Clearances. The much-lamented Highland Clearances culminating in the infamy of Strathnaver in 1814 were only the final sweeping up of a way of life soon to be forgotten except in the songs of romantics and exiles.

These changes took place slowly and erratically under the constraints of topography, access to markets, language (Gaelic or Scots), religion and personal leadership. Nevertheless, with strong forces behind them—'The full influence of the Government, the land owners particularly, the Clergy and even the clan chiefs still left, were all used to extol this new way of life.'(33) They did prevail, to the approval of at least some observers of the period. The 1745 rebellion was 'almost a blessing in disguise' says Andrew Fletcher of Saltoun.(1) Prior to this time roads had been virtually non-existent apart from those constructed by General Wade, and 'the glens and valleys of Scotland had not been a source of young stock of animals or of richness, but a lawless place of poor cultivation and robbery.' Kirk Session Records of the period around 1700 confirm the extreme poverty of the Highlands in particular, from which large numbers of starving men begging from door to door came down to the Lowlands. The old lairds have been blamed for having 'hindered their followers from becoming civilised and have in many way encouraging their idleness'(1) and it has even been claimed by the lowlander 'that large numbers of land-owners themselves were virtually living by robbery, always going armed and doing nothing to cultivate and yield life support from their land'.(1)

In any event, and in the Highlands especially, an old social order had been rent asunder when the battered survivors returned from Culloden Moor; the clan chief—their kin and the object of their loyalty—was likely to be dead, imprisoned, in exile or a hunted refugee in one of his own glens; the clan lands were enclosed, divided and disposed with or without the consent of the absent chief. Again offering a different view Fletcher sheds no tears: 'Bondage built up over centuries was broken to facilitate and be in itself the immediate cause of many material improvements.'(1)

3 THE OLD WAYS

Run-rig

Prior to the eighteenth century the appearance of the Scottish landscape was vastly different from the English scene. This was due not only to the virtual absence of trees in Scotland and the lack of enclosures of any kind but also to the run-rig form of cultivation which covered almost all the areas then in agriculture. This form defies easy description for it has roots in the politics and social organisation of its times, in their technology and also in the nature of the landscape. In those days there was no organised system for maintaining law and order and administering justice. Each baron ruled his own area but had no power beyond it, and a state of virtual anarchy prevailed. Thus it was politic, not only for the landowner but also for his tenants, to have as many people as possible on the land and to have them organised in ways that gave them an incentive to take part in the common defence. One of the ways of achieving this was to divide up the land into a large number of small subsistence units and to intermingle them so that in defending his own land a man could not but defend his neighbour's. Thus run-rig was practically universal in this period when every estate or clan feared the incursions of its neighbours.(12) Conversely when administration of justice became general the run-rig form became unnecessary from that point of view.

Generations of farmers had practised the run-rig system, ploughing the rigs until the huge accumulations of soil attained considerable height: 'The old ridges were nearly as high as they were broad and comprised enormous masses of accumulated earth with uncultivated baulks between the ridges.'(24) Nevertheless the rigs varied in width to an extraordinary degree even

on the same ferm toun. To some extent they were, owing to the
normal action of the plough, more or less the same width from
end to end of the rig, but immovable obstacles such as rocks or
large stones which had to be ploughed around, could change the
width of the rig from one end to the other. The rigs also varied
in height. They could be 5 feet high in the middle for a broad rig
which might extend to 20 yards from baulk to baulk, while others
would be only 3 feet high for a narrow rig 5 yards wide. Nor were
the rigs by any means straight. Generally they ran from top to
bottom of sloping ground and they could be 200 yards long or
more—the longer the better—and were mostly curved to some
degree. Often they had tapered ends curving like an 'S', and
those ploughed by a team of cattle were invariably curved rather
abruptly at either end when the driver had suffered the cattle to
turn too hastily at the rig ends. These limitations were imposed
by the unwieldy nature of the huge Scots plough and the large
team of animals required to pull it.

   But defence and technical factors alone do not fully explain the
continuation for centuries of the run-rigs. Clearly, in the absence
of ditches and tile drains their prime agricultural advantage was
drainage, as the long, high hummocks of the rigs would be
drained by the baulks between them, and the run-rigs were
almost always situated on higher, sloping ground which would
allow water in the baulks to run away into lower pasture area.
Thus the rigs continued not only on heavy clay soils where they
were essential until drainage tiles became available but also in
the upland glens where development was much slower. Baulks
were also useful as access paths for weeding and harvesting
purposes.

   Even when the metal plough arrived the rig system continued,
although the new rigs were more uniform in line and width. Only
the advent of pipe drainage permitted the abandonment of rigs
in favour of ploughing on the level or the contour. This, however,
was not easy for in most cases cross-ploughing of any kind was
quite impossible either on the flat or on steep slopes.(24) The
enormous masses of accumulated earth, with the bare baulks
between littered with stones and rubbish, proved extremely
difficult to level, far less to plough on the contour. Furthermore
the hollows left at the ends of the rigs had become absolutely
barren through the scraping of the plough teams, and water lay

on them much of the time; the only way to deal with them was to cart in soil from elsewhere. (30)

Run-rigs normally varied greatly in size, shape and soil quality, and although by no means a universal practice, they would sometimes be made to change hands yearly. Where this system was practised the individual farmers would cast lots or 'kavels' for their particular share of the rigs. Any portion larger than a normal rig was known as a 'kench'.

The clear division of the ferm toun lands into inbye and outbye areas was a distinctive characteristic of Scottish agriculture up to the end of the eighteenth century. The inbye land was closest to the ferm toun houses and benefited both from the manure produced by man and beast and from the materials used in divot walls and thatched roofs. 'It had been cropped by tillage in bere or oats for centuries, it was a light loam, deep black in colour and easy to work, and was kept free from weeds and was exceedingly fertile.' (20) It also contained to a large degree the top spit or stone-free loam off the adjoining outbye areas.

The outbye land, which was never manured and only ploughed infrequently, was usually more distant from the dwellings. It had been pared of the top spit or divot, the accumulation of grass roots, leaves and tree fibre over thousands of years, which was used to enrich the inbye lands. 'Strong and infertile ... It was generally on declivites and where cultivaton was more difficult.' (30) After it had grown a crop of weeds and grass, the latter could take five or six years, as 'it was ploughed two or three years for oats which were seldom worth the cultivation'. 'The outbye land was typically about four times the size of the inbye but only about one-tenth of its value.' (20) Perhaps a more cogent comment is the estimate that at the end of its spell in crop the outbye could only return at the most five, sometimes only three seeds for every one sown. (20) For an overall view of the countryside and the state of its agriculture it should be noted that until well into the second half of the eighteenth century the cultivated areas were small and totally inadequate for the number of cattle which the farmers tried to raise, and 'the vast extent of the countryside lay uncultivated'. (20)

Summer shielings.

The practice of detached grazing was a very important aspect of life in rural Scotland in the eighteenth century. Apart from the casual grazing of herded animals on unfenced patches of land all over the adjoining countryside and the more regulated practice of grazing on defined common grounds, there were the summer shielings. These were particularly important in the Highland areas as well as in most of the valley parishes. Late in spring or early summer when the crops were sown there was first the closing of the march fence gates against stock and then a general migration of animals and people to the summer shielings. Around the middle of the seventeenth century it was the Baron Courts that fixed the dates for this movement of stock from low ground to the hill pastures. 'All stock had to be outwith the head dyke by lst May. The transfer to the summer shielings took place on lst June and the return after 15th July, all must come home together.'(36) The return date quoted in this case is very early and probably referred to a particular district where the six weeks respite from grazing for the land outwith the head dyke was deemed adequate.

The Rev J Robertson tells us that before the introduction of sheep the remote summer grazings around Callander were occupied in separate lots by the tenants of the estates to which they belonged, as they had earlier been part of their clan possessions. Similarly lowland people would move to a particular valley or hillside, and starting relatively low down would move farther afield to more remote shielings as the grazing was curtailed, revisiting the intermediate grazing ground on their way home. The important factor in these lawless times was the imperative need to keep the stock under immediate personal herding and control.

Behind this practice there was the basic fact that in these times the pasture on hills and mountains was infinitely richer than today. Predators in the form of wolves and men hunting with dogs had prevented the red deer stock from building up to today's hugely destructive numbers, and on hill ground there were until recently many more trees, which encouraged better pasture. Alpine plants, now restricted to rocky cliffs and places inaccessible to sheep, abounded and all the lowland and valley cattle found ample, rich pasturage all summer. Rabbits were unknown and the curse of excessive sheep grazing had not reached the hills, for the few sheep then owned by the farmers had little effect on vegetation, particularly on tree regeneration. Bracken was then uncommon. Thus stock throve during the summer in stark comparison to their life of semi-starvation on lowland areas in winter.

While some of the men and a few of the horses remained in the lowland valleys the bulk of the rural population lived up in the high ground all summer. Some idea of the extent of this exodus can be gauged from The Rev William A Gillies' report from the Kenmore Kirk records that in the mid seventeenth century 'there were 2,300 examinable people in Kenmore Parish' (all such persons in the Kirk's area had to be visited and examined by the Minister periodically) but much of the work had to be done in the winter months 'as most were at the summer shielings in summer'.(36)

The summer houses, light structures of sods and branches of trees, were extremely primitive and very little trace of them remains, apart from a few stones. We can imagine what living conditions were like when we read further that the Minister went to these distant areas of his parish despite the discomfort of 'having to sleep on straw in smokey and disagreeable conditions for ten to twelve days at a time on visitations'.(36) In any event in these rough structures the women, girls and children lived all summer, tending the cattle, making butter and cheese for winter use, and living also on barley and oatmeal which had been carried up in linen sacks from their winter homes. But rough as it may have been, this was no isolated life, for in the absence of roads or wheeled vehicles most travellers preferred the direct path over the hills to the winding valley routes skirting bogs and watercourses. Thus the hill-dwellers saw at least as much of the passing scene as they would in their winter homes, and from June to August a holiday atmosphere prevailed. Around mid August the move to the winter houses would begin, as cold winds, rain and the approach of frost and snow on the hill-tops made life in the shielings less comfortable. By this time too the cattle were fat, the 'profusion of excellent herbage'(20) was diminishing for another year, and the grain harvest in the lowlands was imminent.

Run-rig persisted late into the century, as did communal farming, Robertson writing in the eighteenth century that 'there was still run-rig with two, three or four men yoking their horses together in a plough'.(31) Nevertheless this style of agriculture effectively came to an end in the latter half of the century. Within a period of 50 years the farming unit had altered from numerous family holdings of as little as 3 acres within a ferm toun often first to four or five small farms and eventually to a single farm of 100 to 300 acres, as we know them today, each held by one large farmer aided by the labour of his pendiclers or workers. Since run-rig was the normal scene it was little commented on by the writers of the day. Nevertheless it has not by any means vanished from view. In the first place many examples still exist, mainly on hill pastures which the practice of enclosure failed to reach, although some are in lowland pockets of estate policies and a surprising number in woodlands where the land, instead of being flattened at the time of enclosure for plantations, was left in the old run-rigs. Furthermore, many field boundaries and even roads today still follow the curves of the traditional rigs. But even these are not all the traces of the run-rig times or possibly even the most enduring. The name persists in many areas, as between Airdrie and Edinburgh where place names such as 'Stane rig', 'Grey rig', 'Black rig', 'White rig', 'Lime rig', 'Long rig' and 'Short rig' commemorate the ferm touns of the old system. And Burns' immortal song 'The Rigs o' Barley' certainly did not refer to flat fields but to the high, twisting rigs covered with 'bere' where courting couples could find sanctuary in their curving shapes and high ridges.

Land measures

It is interesting and understandable that the measures used to define land areas in the eighteenth century were not abstract, precise and autonomous but functional and work-related. The unit of arable land was a relatively flexible measure—the 'plough' of land or 'ploughgate'. Essentially this was the size of the old ferm toun, the residence and property of sufficient families to cultivate, communally, an area of ground which, year in year out, could be maintained by one plough team pulling the old Scots plough. This was said to amount to 104 Scots acres (131 acres imperial measure)(12)—enough to support some sixteen families, given free grazing on common lands and access to summer shielings—but it is not entirely clear what land was included in the measure and different people in different places have ascribed different acreages to it. The ploughgate could be divided into four 'horse gangs' of 26 acres or eight 'ox-gates' of 13 acres.

Similarly the measure of uncultivated hill grazing areas was the 'soum', a very old unit based on the winter grazing needs of an individual cow. On the moorland grazing the cattle ran in a common herd and each man's entitlement to this right (his soum) was strictly related to his 'room', the term for his ability to support their winter requirements. The extremely hard conditions and lack of grazing and feed meant that cows calved only every second year and 'followers' could thus be up to three years old.

As regards specific measures the (Scots) acre consisted 6,104 square yards but was subdivided into 4 roods of 1,520 square yards, each rood into 40 falls of 38 square yards, each fall into 36 square ells, the ell being a little over 37 inches long. Incidentally, Panton's map of 1773 (Figure 1) was based on the use of a Scot's chain measuring just over 74 feet imperial measure and divided into 100 links.

4 THE AGRICULTURAL REVOLUTION

Prior to the agricultural revolution of the eighteenth century, life in rural Scotland—and Scotland was rural to all intents and purposes—was governed by two elemental needs: self-defence in a lawless land, and bare subsistence based on agriculture. The social structure and the land tenure system catered for defence; the three-pronged system of agriculture—run-rig cultivation, the distinction between inbye and outbye, and summer shielings—for subsistence. The resulting standard of living, although it varied greatly from area to area, was generally low and precarious: 'They lived an extremely primitive life on what they could grow, content with the coarsest attire, and all their cultivation was carried out with instruments of their own construction.'(12)

Even before 1745 new concepts and practices of agriculture and land management had been evolving—very unevenly, it is true—but the end of the 1745 rebellion released a set of forces which transformed evolution into revolution, so fast was the new rate of change. Probably the major catalyst consisted of the new Board of Agriculture headed by Lord Kames of Blair Drummond, who more than anyone was responsible for accelerating this vast change. Far ahead of his contemporaries his aim was to promote 'the formation of a soil of perpetual or indefinite fertility, artificially, in imitation of some soils found in nature'. 'He aimed at building up soil structure as a main plank of reformed lands.'(1) Once set in motion the new forces made short work of the old order and the run-rig style of cultivation, which had existed for hundreds of years, virtually disappeared within two generations of farming.(30)

One basic factor which facilitated this revolution was the fact that relatively little of the land was under cultivation. There were huge areas of land surplus to the need of the population. Only the best dry areas had been occupied and ploughed, adequate perhaps for the cereal food needs of the people concerned and enough for all that their primitive implements and poor, unfed cattle and horses could cultivate. There is much evidence for this statement. 'The vast extent of the countryside lay uncultivated.'(20) 'From Alyth as one goes to Glenisla there is a tract ten miles long by one mile broad, in which a furrow has never been drawn.'(12) Furthermore Lord Kames cites a huge area between Greenlaw in Berwickshire to Fala in Midlothian 'of Moorland completely unbroken although by 1760 it had a turnpike road running right thro' it, giving access to lime'. Nor was this poor, difficult or inaccessible land. Even in 1775 'particularly fine land' with gravelly subsoil requiring no drainage and close to Perth, a busy seaport town, was still 'in a state of nature'.(35) But in addition land was becoming available from a different source as the Lowland clearances began and displaced possessors, possibly glad to exchange the long hours and poor wages of the new mills for a poor living on the soil, began their exodus from the land.

Another factor in the coming of the revolution was simply that agriculture in Scotland was extremely primitive and begging for improvement. Lord Kames was not the only critic when he said, 'The large area of outfield was entirely uncultivated and was abandoned to the cattle and reduced to thistles and withered straw.'(24) In 1750 Mr Fullerton of Gallerie, who had practical experience of farming methods on both sides of the border, was writing to his friend Mr Hope of Rankeillour: 'I wish Scotland were enclosed, we might then labour as they do in England.'(10) Even more specifically in 1773 Wight was strongly advocating the new idea of dividing the old run-rig landscape into proper farms instead of the miserable narrow strips of rig cultivation, as well as the erection of steading buildings to shelter stock, fodder and grain 'as near the centre of the new farming area as possible'. He also saw the benefit of artificial manures to the impoverished landscape, advocating the use of marl on the summer fallow which, he suggested, should be carried out every fifth year 'to bring the land into a fit state'. And lastly, 'where there was no natural water ditch, hedge boundaries which would be an effective barrier to sheep should be erected'.(35) In passing, the early hedges did not sustain Wight's optimism. The Perthshire parish ministers in *The Statistical Account* report that sheep not only broke through the hedges but in the Parishes of Dron, Moneydie and Tibbermore, ate them! For generations the management of estates had been considered too menial a task for the large landowners, even the exceptions being inclined to preach rather than practice. So there was much to be done in rural Scotland and much scope for doing it. The motive force was that, especially since defence was no longer paramount, some people saw that there was profit to be made from land. Whereas it was then being used to feed large numbers of people inefficiently, with more efficient management and cultivation and fewer mouths on it the land could produce much more money for its owners. This was particularly true of lightly committed lands such as commons and summer grazings. Prominent among those imbued with the new vision were merchants and traders who, having already made money from cheap labour, now turned to the country with offers to rent land from the lairds which the latter could not resist.(12) These new monied farmers then created substantial farms out of the old holdings, fenced and enclosed them and adopted improved farming techniques. Thus they proved that not only could a living be made from the land but its products could also be used in trade to create wealth. The landowners, noting their success and trying to emulate them on their home farms, studied agriculture and took advantage of improved travel opportunities to see for themselves the more advanced practices in England.(12) In short the 'establishment', backed by societies, landowners, merchants, manufacturers and the emerging farmers, was now strongly committed to more intensive cultivation, and great progress was in the offing.

The most deeply significant element in the agricultural revolution was enclosure, for it symbolised change not only in the traditional way of using land but also in the social structure, the land tenure system and the human settlement pattern. Enclosure of land started in Scotland only after the union with England, for the slow build-up of population over the previous centuries had been met by the breaking in of new land and the sub division of existing holdings. Once started it took only some 50 years, from 1740 to 1790, to gain impetus, although even by the latter date two-fifths of the arable land in Scotland was said to be still open and unenclosed.(30)

Prior to enclosure the country was bare of fences, hedges or walls and had few roads and practically no trees. Even the shrubs, whins and gorse, if not burnt for fuel, were eaten down by herds of starving cattle wandering freely during the winter months. Before this there were only the old head dykes, the fences separating the cultivated and hay-bearing part of the area from the hill pasture onto which all animals were turned from May to October. Even today we can sometimes see two such barriers, the lower with fewer stones and the remains of the turf which formed their main construction, the higher entirely of stone and built more recently as the families increased in the valley and more food was required for man and beast.

The building of the enclosures, instigated largely by the landlords, was carried out mostly by the new tenants and at their cost. The old heritable 'possessor' and the insecure 'kindly tenant' are no longer mentioned, for fixed leases were now the rule. Thus in Loch Tayside when the laird started giving leases in 1770 he held the new tenants bound to build stone walls or to provide boundary ditches to the farm and to keep the buildings and walls in repair.(11) Normally, of course walls could only be erected in stoney areas or where sandstone outcrops could be quarried. In Perthshire the enclosures were initially effected by ditches and quickset thorn hedges planted after 'all the land had been broken in'.(33) This confirms that during run-rig times only a minor part of the land was cultivated and that even in areas with free natural drainage and with no boulders or stones much of the land lay uncultivated, being reserved for grazing or hay.

In the glens the new enclosure fences were at right angles to the head dykes, marking the distinction between the emerging new farms and the old ferm touns. These were substantially built walls often contemporary with a new head dyke, in which case the earlier head dyke would be robbed of its stone and often completely obliterated. Normally the new walls were repositories for the ample supply of stones unearthed by cultivation, and some of them incorporated really massive boulders, but in some areas there was a serious stone-disposal problem as distinct from a wall-construction problem. Thus in some stoney and densely populated areas 'consumption dykes', yards wide, were created solely for the disposal of boulders, for to have filled in hollows with them would have wasted grazing area. In lowland areas the construction of the emerging inter-village roads also became a useful outlet for stones removed from the new fields. In some cases the early stone walls were bitterly resisted by the local populace. The practice of enclosure was started in Galloway in 1700 by cattle dealers who sold Scots animals in the English market and realised the benefit of pasturing them in the Border area for a time before sending them south. Mob riots followed these early enclosures, the walls being torn down by enraged rural people who saw this action by incoming entrepreneurs as the end of the traditional free grazing for their few animals. The wrath of the common people, who gathered in large crowds of men, women and children to uproot the hated walls, had to be restrained by the police and even the military were called in to halt the violence.

Since one of the elements destroyed by enclosure was communal working of the land it is scarcely surprising that a second casualty was the commons, and not just the outbye and shieling lands together with the untilled moorland but also lands adjacent to towns and villages which had been used for free grazing from time immemorial. In the days when there was more than enough land for everyone's needs all the local people could graze their limited stock on such areas. Their needs, and with it their grazing rights, were limited however primarily to the production of their milk or transport requirements. And having no cultivable land they had few draught animals. These needs were met by the reservation of a communal grazing area nearby, to which the herd lassies, or the 'Birley Man' sounding his bugle, would drive the cows each morning. There may well have been a link between the feu duty on the house site and the rent of the grazing area, but in fact free grazing was a long established custom and right.

Under the old clan system in Scotland there appear to have been many minor possessors who originally claimed grazing rights on parts of the clan domain, and at the same time there was tacit agreement between adjoining proprietors that a certain proportion of their lands should be reserved for pasture and used in common for the 'mutual convenience of their respective adjoining tenants'.(22) As land increased in value however, these latter areas were envied by the surrounding landowners, so those who controlled the law altered it for their own good. Up to about 1764 the law required the unanimous consent of all commoners 'to the division and enclosure of the divided parts of a common, unless under an act of Parliament'. An eminent lawyer of the time, James Anderson, writing in his 'Essays relating to agriculture and rural affairs' thought this bad, for the following reasons, which throw light on the thinking of the times:

1 The cost of the special Act of Parliament.
2 The difficulty of settling just bounds on the claims of the Lord of the Manor and of the title owners.
3 The cost of fencing (walls or ditches and hedges) of each new plot, as was then required.

. No thought or sympathy was given to the original house owners who lost their ability to keep a cow!

What emerged was a short Act whereby any commons, except those belonging to the King, could be divided at the instance of any individual by a summons raised against all parties concerned before the Lord of Session, who would then divide the common. No persons but the immediately adjoining heritors were allowed to have any share of the common lands. This was based on the assumption that originally every common was considered a constituent part of every adjoining estate. Thus those affected lost their original common grazing right just as urban parishioners could no longer take their souming of cattle to the parish glen lands. Now rents were paid for grazing privileges and these rents were adjusted to take into account not only the actual piece of land the tenant occupied but also any retained right to graze on the common land. This meant that the ownership of the large commons in Scotland might be held by several adjoining lairds, each fencing off his own share, whereas across the border in England a common usually belonged exclusively to one person, the Lord of the Manor.

Another approach to the enclosure of desirable common land arose from the fact that the law was so worded that those wishing to enclose could compel the adjoining proprietor, by means of a process raised before the Sheriff, to 'straight marches' at the sight of the Sheriff. Thus the amalgamation of holdings, the excambion of detached portions of land and the desirability of 'straight marches' all helped to change the old landscape with its crooked boundaries, its ridged and curved parcels of land, and the possession by the same individual of separate pieces of arable land in different farms. All these practices were swept away. The Sheriff had to perambulate the boundaries of the proposed enclosure and was given power to settle the exact lines of the fences, following which the willing and the unwilling parties in dispute had to halve the cost of the march fence! Thus the power of the adjacent heritors over the large commons was well established—based, incidentally, on the valuation of their land and properties. Earlier the right of use had been extended to those who had built houses on feued land within a parcel which had originally held grazing rights, often leading to long wide 'rakes' or 'double dykes', roads leading from towns out to the grazing areas.

The common mosses, as distinct from the common lands, were of less account in that they could still remain in common provided the parties with vested interests did not consider them of sufficient value to divide. Oddly enough we see here the power of moneyed interests emerging to challenge the old principle of the overlordship of the clan chiefs. By this time the opinion of the Laird was strong but only in a negative sense. He often had only a small personal claim on the common lands but he did retain the power to bar or delay their division or enclosure. This particularly referred to tithes, for the greatest obstacle of the process appears to have been the settlement of the Clergy's tithes.

Thus the commons were swallowed up by greedy landowners regardless of old rights and privileges, and the common towns-folk and the ferm toun dwellers both lost their heritage. To the former this certainly meant inconvenience, if not loss; to the latter it meant an end of a pastoral existence. While the individual small farmer might have other land to cultivate, nevertheless he lost his share of the outbye land and the soum on the hill pastures inherited from his forefathers. He now held and worked only the old inbye land of several former possessors. Graziers were also moving onto the estate lands, where their sheep and cattle found easy picking on the old outbye and shieling lands. As a result most of the outlying crofts on fertile hillside patches were obliterated too. Today the occasional ash tree or pile of stones marks the site of not one but five or six families' homes, wiped out by a grazier who could offer money as rent whereas the old crofters had no cash income. As a result of all these actions there were far fewer people on the land, as many as a dozen holdings being reduced to one. The scale of the displacement can be seen from the case of Kilmadock Parish where, in the twenty-five years between 1765 and 1790 the population dropped from just over 800 to about 400 due to the letting of land, and even complete farms, to graziers. This clearance was slow, for only a couple of families were moved out per year, but the end result was dramatic. Most of these displaced moved to the towns, only two families emigrating abroad from this particular parish in this period. This however was the general pattern throughout Scotland.

As another result of all these social and economic forces a great deal of new attention was given to the land, and huge areas were broken in between 1760 and 1780. A mammoth part of this work was the removal of boulders, for large stones were everywhere. With the old wooden Scots plough they had to be avoided at all costs, for hitting a large boulder was likely to shatter the plough, and replacement wood was very hard to come by in the virtual absence of trees. In addition, before the building of stone drains and walls as a means of stone disposal, a great deal of effort and land had always been expended in avoiding boulders. Now with the new values attached to land the inefficiency caused by boulders was no longer tolerable and greater efforts were directed towards their removal. However, labour was plentiful and cheap and gangs of men were employed to remove stones during ploughing operations.(22) In the latter part of the century the introduction of gunpowder was a great step forward, especially since, now that tenants were paying rent in money as well as in kind, the proprietor met the cost of boring holes in the boulders prior to blasting. The boring of the holes was carried out by contract labour which cost one half pence per inch of hole bored.(24) The shattered boulders were then removed by the tenant for use in the new stone field walls and roads.

Even apart from the boulder problem there were the twin difficulties of dealing with the run-rigs and their baulks and breaking in areas which had previously been avoided as being difficult or unprofitable to cultivate. Generally speaking the

rough work of breaking in areas was done by the old Scots
plough, followed by the new metal plough (Small's plough), and
often as many as five cross ploughings were deemed necessary
before crops could be sown. In wet and heavy soils high ridges
were still used to effect drainage. Often two of the Scots ploughs
would follow each other in the same furrow; the leading plough
would have a wide-set mould board, which was still of wood, and
this threw a broad furrow; the second had a narrow mould board
to throw the soil into the furrow of the first one.(22) An
alternative was to omit the second plough and to engage gangs
of men on piece work to help dig the bottom spit. One of the old
plough teams of cattle and horses would be followed by a team
of six to ten men endeavouring to keep pace with the plough—
a truly back-breaking task.

Similarly previously unbroken areas—moorland and
gravelly hillocks for example—would be ploughed in circular or
contour fashion to accommodate the difficulty in turning the
unwieldy Scots plough.

Later in the century turnips were used as the first crop after the
breaking of new ground, followed by oats or barley with clover.
Then too, as times became more settled some estates used a crop
of trees to clear the land by planting Scots pine on poor land
'worth 2d per acre'. Twenty five years later this ground was let
to tenants who paid 10s. per acre for the land and then removed
the trees while the owner got the tree crop.(22)

So during the years following the 1745 rebellion the seeds of
change were planted which were to change the face of rural
Scotland economically, socially and visually. Not all of these
seeds bore immediate fruit; change was sporadic in the extreme
and for many decades primitive and advanced conditions could
exist side by side. The case of the Parish of Udny in
Aberdeenshire in 1790 affords a glimpse of conditions in that
time of transition.

The proprietor of the lands of Udny, a Commissioner of
Excise, contrived to get no less than 400 acres under his own
direct control. This represented four ploughgates, the land
necessary for four ferm touns or some twenty or thirty families.
By 1790 he had been able to enclose 200 of these acres leaving 200
still open but exclusive to his own use. The area was well within
the old hill dyke, so all the new barriers were 'corn fences' or

personal 'parcel' boundaries: (the words wall or dyke were not yet in use for a barrier made exclusively of stones; the term used then was fences). His stock barriers, not so much to enclose as to exclude, were mainly such new stone fences, though in other areas, where stones were scarce, a hawthorn hedge was used. All around him more than half the farm land of the parish was still being ploughed communally in run-rig style using the Scots plough. The remainder, much of which was quite open, was now being enclosed and ploughed with the short English or Small's plough. In Udny Parish this would give, at a rough count, thirty farmers or less using or adapting to the new farming pattern, one large landowner with 400 acres, and some 300 men each with less than 8 acres, cultivating in the old communal run-rig fashion.

Soon the heritors who owned the land, often absentees from the local scene, were giving leases for terms of 19 or 21 years to farmers (their presumed remaining life span) who were by then employing labourers. These were held in bondage by giving them a small area to cultivate for their own food needs and on which to erect their primitive houses. This was described as 'a boll's sowing' (140 pounds of oats or barley) and would cover only a very small area, which would be ploughed for the labourer by the farmer during the winter months. The common man by then had no horse, had lost his inherited grazing rights and was entirely dependent on the farmer, who had also lost his heritage to the Laird. Only landowners, and the larger ones at that, could be termed heritors and it was they who made and enforced the new mode of life. As and when the farmer tenant required labour it was given under compulsion by the labourers who, however, were fed by the farmer's wife during their period of service, thus ensuring that they had adequate sustenance while employed!

Once the farmer's crops were sown the labourers were free to accept day wages if they could obtain work elsewhere. However they were bound to return to the farm immediately their services were required there, and their wives were under similar bondage. They were allowed to keep a cow and a sheep or two to provide wool for the family's clothing and although they had no turf or peat cutting rights of their own they were allowed to strip the top divot off the outbye land as fuel, or to cut peats if a bog was nearby. If they moved to other employment they could not move this fuel, which was the laird's property. They still owned the roof spars and the door of their house—which had no window—but the thatch, which was useful as manure, was the farmer's. They moved, when they could, from farm to farm with no security whatsoever.

Thus proud possessors who had followed their chiefs to battle before the 1745 rebellion were reduced in one generation nearly to slave status. They had never had much land but previously their sons could and did share equally in breaking in and thus 'possessing' a patch on the clan grounds. All this the new system changed, driving 90 per cent of the rural populace from the land and doing it with little protest, for the heritors were dominant.

5 AGENTS OF CHANGE

Dykes and hedges

Although the vast change in rural Scotland in the eighteenth century had institutional roots, especially in land ownership and tenure, change in the landscape itself stemmed from a number of specific technological developments. The most important of these related to dyking, drainage, roads, ploughs, the use of 'marl' and tree planting, and of these the most symbolic—in relation to the idea of enclosure—was dyking. Thus the evolution of boundary barriers, a new departure in Scotland, provides a fascinating insight into the progress of the agricultural revolution.

Most estate boundaries, and in fact many parish and county boundaries, followed natural features. The centre line of a river or stream was and still is a recognised boundary despite its potentially temporary nature—since the course of the river may change. Similarly the crest line of a mountain range often sufficed, later to be marked by post-and-wire fence lines. Walls were seldom built along hill tops although long, laboriously constructed walls built at right angles to the contour tell of a time of cheap labour and a general lack of gainful employment.

The head dykes between the outbye land and the moorland must have been the first artificial boundaries. They were made of easily available material, mainly stone and/or divot, and took full advantage of natural escarpments and cliffs.

In lowland areas, following the loss of the hill grazings, a division was sometimes required between the outbye and the inbye land. However the divisions into what we now call fields were often preceded by small and often circular enclosures within the outbye lands for the overnight retention of stock. Close herding of stock during the summer was the rule and all the animals were either tethered or kept from the crops by young herdsmen or girls. A plentiful supply of children was available before the advent of rural schools and quite young children were employed to look after the cows of childless people. Not only was there a need to keep stock off the grain in the ferm toun lands but the herds had to keep them from encroaching on the unfenced fields of neighbours.

Few of the earliest head dykes were made entirely of stone, most being stone and divot in layers. However the divot available at that time was not an inferior material but a densely packed mass of grass-root fibre established over centuries of growth, that could be cut to shape and was considered a relatively permanent building material. Reflecting this the Statistical Account refers to 'stone fences in Udny which were somewhat new'. Towards the end of the eighteenth century, when the first plantations were 'weeded' (the best of the thinnings went to the Laird) division fences of 'palings of wood were in fact used, but they were weak'.(24) Where stone was not readily available to augment the divot, and in areas where the irreplaceable divot had all been burnt, a good boundary 'was considered to require two ditches and two hedges with a high mound between'.(24) The English 'laid' boundary or division hedge was very seldom used in Scotland.

The construction of stone fences improved. 'Some walls were built of stone $2\frac{1}{4}$ foot high, then a thick sod of grass was laid on, grass side up, the width of the wall. Loose soil was put on top rounded like a ridge then a wide sod placed overall gravelly side up. The upper story was then well beaten by two men, standing on each side of the wall beating it with wooden mells simultaneously.'(24) Since this wall itself could not withstand an active grazing animal additional work was necessary. 'A ditch was then cast on each side, 12 inches from the wall and sloping outwards, to a depth of three feet and four feet wide',(24) thus taking up at least 12 foot width of ground. 'This wall cost 3/- rood of 36 ells and about one seventh the price of a full height stone wall.'(24) (Lord Kames was obviously referring to areas like his home estate at Blair Drummond where stone was none too plentiful.) Ample supplies of cheap manual labour were available and the craft of dry stone walling was yet to attain the degree of skill evident in later examples. Thus 'it was customary to consider that dry stone walls would require a lot of maintenance'.(24)

Soon the early low wall-cum-ditches was superseded and around 1790 efficient dry-stone dykes were being built extensively. For one thing transport was now easier as roads were made for the carting of suitable material (carts instead of panniers or currans being now in use), and much progress was being made in the building of stonewalled houses in general. 'A 6 foot high dyke, extending to 1 rood (36 ells) cost £1. To enclose a 10 acre field cost £150.'(24) On these walls $1\frac{1}{2}$ per cent was the customary allowance for maintenance.(24)

The progress of walling varied from county to county. In the south, where sheep barriers were early required, the 'Galloway dyke' was in use as early at 1720. These 'snap dykes' were of dry stone construction, built three to four feet high, with a few bond stones, then closed on top with a row of coping stones. On top of this coping was built the 'snap', 18 inches height of single stones which tend to tumble and thus deter cattle and sheep.

Although old established hedges are rare in Scotland compared with England, hedges were tried as fences in the late eighteenth century. However, they faced considerable difficulties and many were abandoned as the estates turned to stone walls as a more suitable and permanent alternative. Around 1770 both private and estate nurseries grew thousands of hawthorn plants to surround the new enclosed fields. The nurseries were protected by ditches and snap dykes. The new wood plantation thinnings were used to provide protective fences for the young plants in the new hedges. Despite this protection many hedges were destroyed by cattle and even more by sheep, to the extent that some estates and even whole lowland parishes had to ban sheep altogether. Even the introduction of skilled men from England to 'plash' the growing hedges failed to establish them as effective stock barriers.

Drainage

The main fact governing agriculture—and in fact the total appearance of the countryside—in the first half of the eighteenth century was the complete lack of underground drainage. Drain

tiles had not yet been invented; it was not until 1826 that the first
tile works in Scotland were built at Cessnock, Ayrshire, by the
Duke of Portland. Thus vast areas were quite impossible to
cultivate and remained as meadow land often shared by all as
'common bogg' and cut for hay when the animals were absent at
the shielings in summer. As distinct from today's pattern of
normally rectangular fields the landscape then featured
innumerable irregular arable islands in a sea of boggy or 'riske'
land, as it was then termed.

In cultivated lands surface water was shed into hollows and
natural water courses from the high curving ridges by the baulks
of the run-rigs. Seepage and spring water had to be controlled in
a different manner—by open ditches or 'hollow drains', a
development which preceded the invention of drain tiles. These
were shallow tracks often formed by the plough, filled with
stones, brushwood or straw, covered over, and then led into open
ditches or natural streams. By 1790 Patrick Cruickshank of
Stracathro in Strathmore was laying open drains 6 feet wide at
the top, 1 foot wide at the bottom and 3 feet deep. These cost 10d.
to 1s. per rood whereas covered drains, which were only 18
inches wide and 2 to 3 feet deep, were much cheaper to construct—only 3d. a rood.

In addition to marshy lands, shallow lochs and water-covered
areas were also becoming subjects for drainage, sometimes for
land reclamation, sometimes to permit the removal of marl from
the loch beds for use as fertiliser. Thus the Rev J Robertson tells
of Mr Buchan of Cambusmore draining 10 feet off Loch Lubnaig
in West Perthshire to reclaim 50 acres of land at the head of the
loch.

By far the most extensive scheme of land drainage in Scotland
took place on Blair Drummond Moss in West Perthshire where
thousands of acres of estuarial clay land lay buried under 8 to 20
feet of peat moss. The clearing of this huge area is vividly told in
Cadells' *Story of the Forth* and also in the *General view of the Southern
Areas of Perthshire* written less than thirty years after the work
began. Shallow drains, 2 feet wide at the start, were gradually
deepened as the work proceeded in the moss. A stream was
diverted into these trenches into which the peat was hand-cast by
spade to flow eventually out into the Forth estuary. Whole
families set at this work managed eventually to expose small

areas of the underlying fertile clay for cultivation and by 1783, after seventeen years, forty-two tenants had cleared their portions of 8 acres each, sufficient in these times to provide a livelihood. In clearing 336 acres in this way however, they had exhausted the stream. Then the brilliant idea of utilising a 'Persian Wheel' to raise water from an upstream part of the Forth River was devised by Blair Drummond Estates and this diverted a more adequate and reliable flow of water into the reclamation area. Within four years no less than fifty-five additional families had taken advantage of the new facilities to settle on the Moss.

The Persian Wheel was built in Alloa by Meikle, 28 feet in diameter and '10 foot broad on the flat boards'. This raised 40 hogshead (2,000 gallons) of water per minute 17 feet to an elevation 2 feet above the moss level. Then 18 inch diameter wooden pipes conveyed the water first in an underground trench 354 yards long through a cutting and thence by open aqueduct to the moss. The £11,000 cost of the wheel had to be met by the tenants on a loan basis; the Laird however cut the new road onto this part of the moss and met the loan charges on the wheel.

The early settlers, mainly from the Western Isles, who when they first arrived seventeen years earlier had lived in hovels excavated in the peat, had by this time built brick houses roofed with straw. The land was squared off by the drainage ditches and parallel to these were the access roads. Those roads remaining are still called 'lanes' and are named after some of the more prominent original settlers.

There were two distinct settlement levels on the reclaimed Moss, and comparison of the earlier settlement leases with those undertaken by their successors demonstrates the rapid evolution of rent from payment in kind to cash settlements. The first settlers, who required no capital investment, got 38-year leases. They paid no rent for seven years and in the first year they received two bolls of meal as well as timber for the roofs of their primitive shelters. On the expiry of the eighth year they paid 1 merk (13s.4d. Scots) per acre of their holding, much of which was still to be cleared of peat. Each year thereafter the rent increased by 1 merk per acre until by the nineteenth year they were paying 19 merks per acre. From the fourteenth to the nineteenth year they also paid one hen for each acre. By this time it was considered that they should have cleared their 8 acre farm and for the following nineteen years they paid 12 shillings for every cleared acre and 2s.6d. for every acre still uncultivated, the yearly hen levy also being increased to two hens per acre. The Estate's method of dealing with 672 hens on rent day is not recorded!

The settlers on the high moss, who had to meet the loan charges on the wooden pipe aqueduct, paid no rent for the first nineteen years, following which they paid the same rent as the earlier settlers on the low moss. By this time the latter had to face new terms and no doubt the hen levy was omitted from their lease since up to 600 hens per annum were now coming in from the second development. Soon the roll call of the reclaimed lands comprised 115 men, 113 women, 119 boys, 193 girls, 115 cows, 35 horses and carts. A total of 300 acres had been cleared and the grain crop raised to 8 bolls per acre. At this date there was still only one horse and cart for every three farms and one cow per family was the rule.

There was a further area, the 'slow' or 'flow' moss on which not even temporary houses could be built, and this was let out to the high moss tenants for clearing in 8 acre plots, by payment of £12 advanced to each at 5s. per cent interest per acre. Prizes were given by the Estate to encourage development: the tenant clearing the most moss down to the clay was given a plough, the second a wheelbarrow, the third a spade plus ten pounds of clover seed. The community now merited a school, which was aided by a grant from Edinburgh of £10, and a house was built for the master, who received £5 per annum from the estate. The effect of the gross pollution of the River Forth is unrecorded, but it is known that a Mr Dundas of Blair near Culross used water-borne peat deposited on the foreshore nearby as a compost on his land along with dung.(31)

Roads

Prior to the rebellion in 1745 there was little need for roads in rural areas and as a result there were very few, the main ones being General Wade's military roads constructed some ten to twenty years earlier. By 1734 Wade had constructed the

Stirling–Crieff–Aberfeldy Road and the road from Callander by the east side of Loch Dochart through Strathfillan over the Black Mount to Fort William. Furthermore a link had been made between them over the hill from Lochearnhead to Ardeonaig, and the third Earl of Breadalbane had made a road from Kenmore to Glendochart on the north side of Loch Tay.

Not having been designed for inter-community use these roads were not used much more than the old hill tracks and foot-and-horse-paths they superseded. The rural dweller as he was then had no need for wheeled transport; grain was only grown for family needs and was not sold off the farm except in the vicinity of towns or seaports. Grain used for whisky was carried in hand-woven linen sacks on horseback and the end product in bladders, casks or earthenware jars from Europe. As the modern generation use Spanish and Portugese sherry casks for whisky transportation as well as storage, so did the early eighteenth century use the 'Grey beard' jars of the Rhenish towns, originally used for wine, as poteen containers. The Laird may have brought them over for his own use but they were much more important when recycled! The 'Bellarmine' jars bearing the effigy of the Cardinal are found in all sorts of unlikely places in the Angus glens. In short anything going to mill or market had to be carried on horseback. Such grain and fuel as were transported were carried mainly in pannier 'creels', or occasionally borne on a frame of sticks dragged by a horse. In the same vein in 1765 McArthur tells of the coals for Taymouth Castle being carried on horse creels from the pits in Clackmannan via Crieff to Kenmore.(11) Needless to say, all personal travel was done on horseback.

It was only when the original subsistence holdings were amalgamated into larger farms that the dominant farmer then had grain to dispose of, and when the villages and towns grew large enough to need the produce, roads for transporting it became necessary. Then as the principal landowners began to use wheeled vehicles and as trade increased the defects of the system became ever more apparent. 'The Angus roads were narrow, rugged, winding and steep'; 'sufficient width for a horse with panniers was adequate indeed'.(12) And since all the roads in rural areas were quite impassable for wheeled transport from November to March 'wheel carriages were little used except in

the most cultivated parts'.(12) In the towns the use of carts
became possible as the principal routes were stone-paved. Only
a light paving or stone flags without much in the way of
bottoming was used in the early days, and while this was
adequate for foot or horse passage it soon proved inadequate for
the increasing number of wheeled vehicles. When these were
used for the first time in the City of Aberdeen around 1730 they
'cut up the causeways and converted them into roads which lay
deep in myre all winter and in deep dust all summer to the
annoyance of the inhabitants'.(33) It was almost a generation
later, in 1750, before any attempt was made to form roads in the
rural parts of Aberdeen. In 1794, 'it was still impossible to drag
a wheeled carriage with any more than half a load owing to the
atrocious surfaces'.(13) ('The load of a country cart is about 7
cwt.'(4)) Thus the development of roads and vehicles proceeded
in a somewhat sporadic manner across the country over quite a
considerable period, but by the second half of the century the
lines of most roads had been defined.

Roads in rural areas were being started around 1760,
constructed, as the early farms had been, by the use of that
solitary piece of mechanical equipment, the old Scots plough.
Farmers banded together to plough a strip of land through and
round the early settlements. This was originally lined out 30 foot
wide. It was ploughed again and again towards the centre like a
long wide run-rig snaking through the parish. When the centre
parts stood about 2 feet high in a width of 12 feet it was covered
with gravel or broken stone. It was thus only after the middle of
the century that the use of carts in rural areas could even be
contemplated. However their use became common with the
spread from Ayrshire of an important new development in road
construction. Whereas the Romans had constructed paved
roads and laid foundations of brushwood in boggy areas, more
recent roadmakers including Wade had based their roads on any
readily available boulders or rock. John MacAdam of Ayrshire,
returning to his homeland from America in 1777, invented an
entirely different road building method. This involved the
construction of a road surface of sufficient elasticity to give
slightly to heavy loads and yet return to a level surface. The
MacAdam road surface was built to a slight camber with 12
inches of broken stone of uniform size; no particular bottoming

was called for. The roadmen were issued with a 2-inch diameter ring and a 6-ounce balance to ensure uniformity, and granite stone was specified if obtainable, no sand or dressing admixture being allowed. MacAdam soon became notable as a road trustee and ultimately became Deputy Lieutenant of Ayr County (in which capacity he raised a force of Fencibles to defend the country when threatened with invasion by France). He and his three sons could claim to have been the founders of the Scottish road system, and his own driveway, laid out in the new system, was copied by the new road authorities all over Scotland.

When the necessity for roads came to be seen there was no centralised authority to see to their construction and maintenance. After such authority was formed individual farmers nearby with their servants and horses, and individual house holders in the villages, were 'impressed' for a fixed number of days in a year to assist the contractor. This was only practical when the farms had grown to a size that necessitated the employment of labour, but even so the employed labour directed to this work was seldom willing, and little work was done. In the Highlands the clan system, which called for loyalty to fight an aggressor or to join a foraging ploy, was not a satisfactory source of forced labour for road making especially when these same clans would, as they saw it, be far better off without roads! In due course, however, the idea of making the user pay for roads and their upkeep took hold, and in 1790 the landed proprietors of Angus applied for permission to construct 'subscription' roads. These, which were to run to and from the five burghs and the two principal villages, were constructed and were 'in high repair by 1794'.(12) They were stipulated to be 36 feet wide, with cross gradient of not more than 1 in 20. To cover the costs of construction, maintenance and interest charges, tolls were levied every six miles, these charges amounting to 3s. for a saddle horse and 1d. for a two horse cart.(4) These were collected by tollkeepers who bid annually for the right to do so. Any deficit had to be met by statute labour funded by the new tenant farmers.

The construction of side roads from the glens through the country districts and to and from the villages, all leading to the main subscription roads, was carried out by statute labour. To meet these costs a tax of 24s. on every £100 Scots valuation was levied, not on the landowners but on the tenants, a further inducement for the landowners to arrange for more cash-paying tenancies and thus ease their own burdens. However, the technique of statute labour for the construction of the secondary roads proved such a burden, first on the tenant farmers and then on the householders, that in Duns around 1783 statute labour for roads was changed to a road rate.(33) Each house was levied an annual rate of 7s.6d. and each householder had to pay 3s. The interesting difference in rating between householders and houses was a reflection on the change over from the earlier system to the new one. By the new arrangement 'a 2-pair farm (one using four work horses) would pay 33s. or 33 days of labourers pay'.(33) In Aberdeenshire, when the taxing system of farm valuation had proved inadequate, causing the burden to be passed further down the line to the individual householders, the Statute Labour Act compelled every householder to work six days a year on the roads.

Turnpike building had problems in addition to financing, for their progress depended on the co-operation of the landowners through whose estates the roads were planned to pass, and this was not always forthcoming. Nevertheless progress was made and in 1794 Anderson, was writing that 'carriages were passing every minute',(13) although in his youth around the middle of the century twelve pack horses travelling once a week could carry all the commerce between the two principal cities in Scotland, and he could recall a time when 'the presence of a wheeled vehicle of any kind on the road between Edinburgh and Glasgow was such a rarity that the whole village turned out to look at it and the children followed it for a mile'. Robertson also reports that in 1794 there was a road 'nearly finished as a turnpike between Perth and Crieff but not yet between Stirling and Crieff.' It had only just been agreed to make the road and as toll values had not been fixed the scheme was held up. The Stirling-to-Fort William road, which, was of strategic and military value, 'was in good order'.(31)

Other areas were not progressing so well however, and Donaldson reported that before 1794 the Keith-to-Fochabers road, made by the Earl of Findlater, was in very poor order. 'It is really in the highest degree dangerous for strangers to attempt to travel from Keith to Fochabers in Winter.'(15) He further confirmed that at that time the roads from the seaports to the interior were for the most part impassable in winter. In particular he commented on the poor condition of the road through Glendevon from Auchterarder to Blairingone, which was by this date the main trafficway for coal. With the shortage of timber, the depletion of the peat sources and the consumption of most of the hillside topsoil as burning fuel, coal was being carted in small horse-carts through this glen and the road was consequently in very poor order. At that date the further extension of this coal artery to the northern areas was not by the present route from the Braco-Muthill road to Comrie but by a road, now obsolete, through Glen Leightorn, a tributory of the River Knaik. Along this road horse carts carried coal northwards and lime southwards from the quarry on Lochearnside. Incidentally, an excerpt from papers on the coal trade gives an inkling of the value of the development of roads to commerce. Whereas at an earlier date all coals were brought to Edinburgh in wicker panniers on horses' backs, the load for each animal being two hundredweights, by 1794 wheeled carts were in regular use instead, each cart carrying 28 hundredweights. The turnpike toll on this route was $2\frac{1}{2}d$. for each load.

Despite chaos and lack of any practical distribution network, the road commissioners (mainly landowners and other interested parties) were hard at work. The Edinburgh turnpike roads were in shape and the toll-keepers were collecting the necessary revenue and bidding ever increasing sums for that privilege. The Lothians were now levying a tax not only on houses but on land, this amounting from 12s. to 16s. on the ploughgate (in this area 70 acres). In the northern counties where the tax system simply did not work owing to the long distances relative to low valuation, MacKenzie recalls that even up to the potato famine in 1845–8 there were no public roads beyond Auchnasheen and Kinlochewe. What roads there were had been built mainly by the estates concerned; there were no wheeled vehicles at all;(27) and even at that late date sledges were in general use round the townships. Nevertheless the eighteenth century saw the beginnings of a national transport system where none had existed previously.

Marl and lime

The very limited amount of ground cultivated by the run-rig possessors remained reasonably fertile since it lay close to their homes and had the waste material from the family and from the family cow spread on it each spring. Periodically it also received the soot-impregnated roof thatch of straw and divot: and lastly the ashes from the house fire of wood, peat or feal went, along with the household waste, into the midden in front of the door and were also spread on this ground. The outbye land was a more difficult problem. It was too onerous to carry dung to it on the human back and moreover the available dung was barely sufficient for the inbye rigs. However the outbye could be enclosed into small parks called folds to concentrate the deposit of animal manure, while the top layer of adjoining moor land was often burnt and spread on it too. In addition the scraping of the subsoil from the baulks onto the ever-rising masses of earth on the rigs brought basic trace elements into the cultivation layers. Thus since this appeared to be beneficial, and as the outbye land was enclosed and cultivated periodically, efforts were made to spread on it subsoil material from other selected areas. Most of the soil was already acid, indeed too acid, and some effort had to be made to make it more alkaline. Although peat is a fine soil improver with the addition of some lime, the complete absence of lime in the early part of the century meant that the surface peat layers were never utilised and in fact much effort was made to get rid of it.(24)

The imported subsoil which was spread on these newly cultivated lands, the first of the 'artificial' manures, was given the general title of 'Marl'. Under the peat moss of the Carse of Stirling, then being cleared and dumped into the River Forth, was found 'Shell Marl', and this white material was spread on the clay land nearby with astonishing results. No one knew its origin but since it was known that peat was vegetation and the remains of old woodland, the new material was considered to be 'the alkaline salt of rotten wood'.(24) Furthermore its value was considered to lie in its ability to extract oil from the soil! At this time, 1760, marl was also used to extract grease from wool, and so there arose the curious fallacy that 'since marl could extract grease out of wool, being a species of oil, therefore marl on the land could extract oil out of the land'.(24) The term 'shell lime' is still the colloquial term for unslaked lime, a throw-back to the days when marl itself, a shell-like material, was burnt for lime instead of limestone. Thus Headrick of Dunnichen in 1813 was quite emphatic that 'shell marl was formed of small wilks which lived only one year and which multiplied prodigiously'.(18)

The impact of marl as a fertiliser during the enclosures period was tremendous. It preceded and thus fostered the early use of lime, so much needed to correct the original acidity of the soil, and released fertility which maintained the food supply. This was followed by guano from Peru, nitrogen from coal gas conversion and eventually phosphatic and other mineral deposits. During the second half of the eighteenth century the search for marl was exhaustive. One of the references to this new fertiliser was in the works of the Rev Rodger. Writing near the end of the century, he claimed that around 1730–6 a Mr Pearson, had discovered marl in Balgavies Loch near Rescobie in Angus. A Capt Strachan then bought the estate and set to work to mine it by a technique he had seen used to remove ballast from the River Thames. In this fashion the marl was dragged from the shallow loch and used to immense advantage on the surrounding fields. His methods, however primitive, gave him a surplus to sell to his neighbours and excited much interest. Thus the search was on to find this remarkable material.

The shallow meres and lochs of Perthshire and Angus were first exploited, and one of the earliest was Whitefield near County Angus, now fertile farm land. Other lochs drained in Strathmore were Rescobie near Forfar and the Monks Myre, a pond also near Coupar Angus, described by Wright around 1770 as a great source of marl and "a centre of marl digging". At that date he was saying 'Whitefield moss was almost exhausted' and 'thousands of pounds worth of marl have been got here and carried up to ten miles away'.(35) In central and West Perthshire marl was found in great quantities from Auchtertyre to Gask and from Gleneagles to Ardoch.(31)

In Angus, at the instigation of the Earl of Strathmore the level of Forfar Loch was lowered by 16 feet (the north and south ends of the town are built on this reclaimed land) and the outflowing River Dean was excavated some miles downstream to Glamis. Barges were constructed and anchored, with scoops to remove the underwater marl. In this loch, a 'kettle hole' relic of the Strathmore ice sheet, the marl was of pure quality, being free from any mud or peat overlay. Nearby Restenneth Loch, which exposed 120 acres of marl 18 inches to 2 feet deep, was then drained at a cost of £2,000, this being more expensive to remove since it was covered by a bed of peat moss. The sale of this material brought in £3,600 giving a good margin of profit. Following that the nearby Lochs of Rescobie and Balgavies were drained by boat and scoop. 'The dragging cost 3d. to 4d. per boll of 8 cub. ft. and the marl sold for 1/- per boll.'

The marl from these drained lochs, a soft, easily crumbled material which would soon become almost rock-like on exposure to air, was in keen demand by the now well established commercial farms carved out of the old subsistence agricultural scene. As much as 60 bolls (120 bushels or about 20 cubic yards) of marl were applied to an acre of land as an initial application, and some farmers applied an excess of the material, to the detriment rather than the improvement of their soil. So beneficial was this new material that the Angus estates, now busy clearing people off the small farming units and letting the larger farms at enhanced rents would make a point of advising potential tenants of the distance of the farm from the site of the marl.

Another of the early areas to be exploited was the large loch of Kinnordy near Kirriemuir. There disbanded Highlanders wandering the countryside after Culloden, starving men whose old possession of land from the clan grounds had been taken from them by the Commissioners of the Forfeited Estates, were glad to accept work at four pence per day. Working like slaves in the long cut from the Loch to the 'Slade' at Kirriemuir they carried with them dry oatmeal which, dampened from the water in the ditch, was their sole sustenance. As a result of their labours a huge deposit of 300 acres of shell marl was exposed which was still being exploited as late as 1809.(12)

One of the last of these natural deposits to be worked out was Lundie Loch, which, being impossible to drain by open cut, was emptied sufficiently to get at the marl by means of a tunnel blasted by gunpowder. Its excavation in 1809 revealed 40 acres of good marl under a covering of moss and mud, and as a bonus, fuel was produced from the peat layer overlying the marl.

Apart from these decidedly heroic schemes, marl was now being appreciated and sought in more mundane circumstances. Thus in 1773 Robert Ainslie was rather floridly reporting to Thomas Graham of Belgowan (later General Graham and Lord Lynedoch) that he should 'improve the fields and cultivate the genius of the people for the happiness of both proprietor and tenant, an increase of wealth to both and a beauty to the country'. Urging the enclosure of uncultivated lands he particularly advised that before any farm was let, the owner 'should search the whole fields for marl or other manures'.(5) In fact several such deposits were found and exploited without any trace today or any memory of their being.

All this easily accessible fertiliser gave the Angus and Perthshire farmers and landowners a decided advantage over those in other Scottish counties, who had to turn to other means to promote fertility. Where the profit was ploughed back into the land the marl left a legacy in well-built farmhouses and steadings and enabled the larger lairds to promote their standing in England and at court. The improved fertility of the areas dressed with this fertiliser was remarkable; 'Around Muthill area, when the fields were enclosed, the returns with marl were four bolls to every boll sown.'(35) But there was another side to it. At 1s. a boll (the price at Rescobie and Balgavies) 8 cubic feet of this lime-based fertiliser, a large bagful, cost the equivalent of a labourer's wage for a working day of 10 to 12 hours. Quite an expensive fertiliser in social terms!

Areas lacking this handy fertiliser tried other materials, not always with success. 'In Kirkhill Parish, Inverness-shire, where there was no lime or marl, gravel was dug in pits and mixed with the dung.' 'This deformed the countryside and spoiled the pasture'.(33) About 1745 limestone burnt locally in small lime kilns, began to be used for farming.(31) Although not so good as the natural marl, it quickly came into general use and eventually, as supplies of marl began to run out, supplanted it entirely.

At one time all the farms within reach of a limestone outcrop had their kilns, almost to the extent of each farmer or estate producing home-made lime, but soon Forfar lime was being carted into Perthshire where it sold for 42d. per boll. The local lime quarries held their own for a period and in some cases they sold the limestone direct to the farmers, who in turn 'broke it to the size of a turkey's egg and burnt it with peat and timber'.(31) One such quarry of good limestone was opened on the shores of Loch Earn near Lochearnhead in Perthshire. The quarried stone was carted the short distance to the lochside where boats were used to float it down to St Fillans, a distance of ten miles. There it was off-loaded and carted as far as practicable. However fuel for the kilns was soon scarce in this area while transport caused the cost to rise. In an effort to overcome this handicap a canal was proposed from St Fillans to Perth so that cheap barge transport to the market area could be arranged. However, the importation of cheap lime by sea to Perth harbour from Sunderland aborted this proposal and apart from supplying a few local needs the quarry soon fell into disuse. Lime produced at Loch Earn cost 26d. per boll, being much cheaper by this time than marl at 84d. per boll. Limestone was also quarried at Callander, Muckart, Fossaway and Aberfoyle.

Around 20 to 40 bolls of lime an acre was applied to normal soils and 50 to 70 on clay soils, this being approximately the same as marl usage. The new agricultural developers applied both forms of lime enthusiastically and in some cases to excess. For example, it is known that in the Meigle area excessive marl application made the soils so buoyant that wind-blown erosion took place, while Berwick County reported that 'the use of lime was so excessive that streams, formerly full of trout and salmon were now empty owing to the "burning of the fields" '.(33)

Trees

In very early times most of Scotland was tree-clad, natural regeneration being more or less unhampered by animals. The various deer—red, roe or caribou—were held in check by wolves and foxes. There were no rabbits (an introduced species); hares could have had relatively little ecological effect and along with voles were held well in check by these same predators. Tree species in post-glacial times were few—Scots pine, birch, oak, alder, willow, ash, holly, yew, juniper, aspen, bird cherry and rowan. There were no beech, chestnut, plane or even spruces or Norway pine among the conifers. On the moorlands up to 1,000 feet Scots pines were supreme; oaks were found in the river valleys, ash in alkaline soils, and birch and alder woods in the extensive bog lands.

As time went on the increasing human population pressure outpaced regeneration; then clear felling and scrub removal took place as men sought to diversify the predominately fish and shellfish diet of their forefathers with cereals supplemented by whatever animals or birds they could trap, catch or domesticate. Then early man began to use the native, self-sown woods not only for fuel but to provide shelter and boats, and soon trees were confined to the hills, moors and rocky areas. In addition as successive races colonised and replaced earlier peoples the original woods were often destroyed by burning to facilitate the elimination of enemies and in later times, wolves. Still later, charcoal burning removed a great deal, and by the fifteenth century it was apparent that something must be done to replace this rapidly diminishing natural resource.

Thus in 1467 the Scottish Parliament ordained, 'The Kings freeholders shall order their tenants to plant woods and trees and to make hedges under such a penalty as the Lord or Baron shall modify.' Whether the Barons really cared or the tenants tried hard is not known, but the law was quite ineffective and two generations later, in 1534, another national effort was made: 'Any man with land of £100 (Scots) value (£8.6s.8d. sterling) shall, where no woods exist, plant three acres of timber', and 'Tenants to plant one tree for every merks value of land'. Neither law had much effect but a few planted trees did survive and their seedling successors mark the site of some old biggins on the hillsides.

Charcoal burning began. Around Perth there is evidence in several fields, on Pitmurthly Farm at Redgorton, near Methven, and again beyond Stanley, of the presence of charcoal burners' activity. The ground on these sites is still densely impregnated with fine charcoal fragments, the almost indestructible condition of scorched wood, which show up as a dark patch each spring after ploughing. We know that by 1600 on the West Coast Sir George Hay had cut down all the oak trees his contractors could reach and transport for his furnaces or bloomeries.(27) At that date it paid to take the iron ore by ship to the fuel source rather than cart the fuel to the ore deposits. So by 1661

Parliament again spoke: 'Every heritor, life rentor or wad-settor worth £1000 of rent shall enclose for ten years at least 4 acres annually and plant this with trees and others, more or less as to rental value'; 'These plots to be free of all burdens and quartering of horse for 19 years from the date of the Act.' Furthermore 'Anyone cutting a planted tree to be fined £10 or to work for one year to the person injured for meat and drink only.'(30) This severe penalty which could be imposed by the landlords' 'Baron Court', continued and for a hundred years or more no tenant had a right to cut down any planted tree on his farm. The natural woods however were still fair game for anyone. McArthur in 1769 confirms that the tenants in Breadalbane above Aberfeldy had the right, along with mosscutting for fuel, to get timber off the hill, 'since the woods were being cut down for the service of the country'! As a result, by the 1745 rebellion the lowland countryside was completely denuded. It has been recorded in fact that not a single tree could be seen in a day's journey from Stirling to Perth!(24)

With the old landowners exiled the Commissioners set about remedying matters, and this they could do because in the bestowal of estate lands they could, and did, favour those who could and would plant trees. 'Loyal' landowners followed enthusiastically and were supported in turn by the farmers—those in the Carse of Stirling, for example, who by 1790 were setting aside one acre for trees from their holdings of 100 to 200 acres. The practice spread rapidly and the parish Ministers writing in the *Statistical Account of Morayshire* in 1790 commented that in some enclosures planted firs were then large enough to be made into roof timbers. In addition, the planting started during this period not only of conifers but also of deciduous trees, would evolve in time into one of the most distinctive and valuable aspects of the Scottish landscape. The first of these plantations existing or proposed were prominently shown in Roy's map of Scotland in 1750.

In passing, neither the difficulty faced by the early tree planting nor the contribution it has made to the tolerability of the Scottish climate should be minimised. In the almost total absence of trees at that time the winds were fierce and the countryside was windswept to a degree difficult to appreciate today which, incidentally, should make us fearful of the potential effects of current tree and hedge-clearing practices. As a result effective tree-planting at this stage was extremely difficult and according to Lord Kames the foresters had to plough three furrows, one on top of the other, and then set up the divots to form a low wall, north to south. On the east side of these walls some 3,000 trees per acre were planted, almost 3 feet apart, for 'so strong were the winds that otherwise than in the shelter of these walls, tree growth was inhibited'. (24) The low moorland around Lord Kames' home in the Blair Drummond area near Stirling became Scotland's first experimental plantations, and they were widely copied. The first planting was of soft wood—native pines followed soon by Norwegian spruces and Canadian and American firs, and in their shelter hard woods—beech, sycamore, chestnut, both horse and sweet types, imported from the south were planted in their turn. Wherever there were trees the winter climate gradually changed.

A tree now common in the Scottish landscape appeared when, only two or three years before the Atholl men followed Bonnie Prince Charlie, a few seeds of larch trees were imported from Austria, and in 1741 the first two larches to be seen in Britain were planted near the Cathedral at Dunkeld. Some fifty years later, in 1793, Mr Scougall the gardener reported of two planted in 1743 as being 120 feet high, $3\frac{1}{2}$ feet diameter one yard from the ground and containing 110 cubic feet of wood.(22) The second sowing of the original larches had outstripped the first as the former were then only 85 feet high! The 'Planting Duke' was very pleased with his new hobby and three years thence Mr Scougall saw his foresters planting 100,000 larch trees per annum, a degree of foresight for which the Laird's successor was soon to be thankful as it saved him some difficulty in meeting gambling debts at London card tables! The Rev Rodger, who wrote the 'General View of the County of Angus' in 1794, commented on how the Angus lairds had followed the Duke's example: 'The seats of Charles Wedderburn of Pearsie in Glen Prosen, and at Balnaboth nearby and the Castle of the Earl of Airlie at Cortachy showed up as paradises in the surrounding desert of tree-less land due to the planting of trees around the residences.' Later at Cortachy the 'American Garden' was planted with specimen trees by visiting notables. Despite the fact that by this time 12,000 acres of Angus had been planted, the trees around these famous mansions stood out from the native alders and birches—all that had survived near the rivers in that area. In this period wood was put to many uses. The native Scots pines had long since disappeared from the Lowlands since even a 5 inch diameter tree was quickly snapped up as a cart axle, while the gnarled oaks had gone to form cruik trusses for the rural cottages. The dockyards, hard at work on wooden ships, took all the better crooked timber, already shaped by nature to suitable curves, for boat ribs. The towns took the straight young ash and oak timber for furniture and wheel spokes. All the rest was made into charcoal for the foundries, although within a short space of time coal rather than oak was being used to produce steel. Timber prices per cubic foot prevailing in 1794 were as follows:(16)

> Plane: 1/- to 2/- for print fields etc.;
> Beech: 1/- to 2/- for ship keels (if large enough);
>   10d to 1/- for furniture;
> Scots Fir (pine): 6d to 8d

One important product was bark for tanning. While native scrub oak prevailed in the valleys of the Grampians, on lowland hillsides young oaks from English acorns were planted to form copses which were cut every 25 years for bark for the tanneries. Prior to this, birch bark had been used for tanning, even willows and rowans being so used.(31) Cutting of these young oaks started early in May as the sap rose, and by the end of May the felling contractors had taken their harvest since work after that date would have meant that the ensuing shoots, the future crop, would be frosted. The bark, valued at 1s.6d. per stone (measured in 'iron weight'), was removed and carried to the tanners on the coast. Most of the oak woods of Perth and Angus today are survivors of these tanning copses, as can be seen on close examination of the butts, where evidence of the stump growth is apparent.

At one point Moray County had a steady supply of Scots pine forest wood floated down the Spey and to a lesser extent the Tay was similarly used in Perthshire, where the old Caledonian Forest had been exploited even earlier. But by 1794 a small quantity of planted Scots pine timber was coming into use and all the proprietors were planting timber to try to compete with Baltic timber coming into the country. And as the new rectangular fields were marked by stone walls or newly planted hedges, they were outlined at regular intervals by the Laird's trees, which would be cut down in due course to provide a bonus to him. Woe betide the tenant who let his stock damage these trees, for although they might feed off the tenant's land and shade his crops, they were the Laird's property. For the past 200 years rural people have maintained a strong distinction between a planted tree and a naturally sown one, the latter being considered fair game for anyone! This is an interesting relic of the early eighteenth century, where on clan grounds the woods and mosses were considered to be freely available to those of the clan or parish.

Ploughs

There is little doubt that virtually the whole surface of agricultural Scotland was fashioned by the 'Scots Plough', for this strong though primitive implement was used universally to break in new land and to form the long curved ridges on which, up to 1700–1800 all crops were grown. It is ironic that while some of these ridges, though much reduced by weathering, may still be visible to the discerning eye, only one or two of the implements that shaped them have survived, notably one now in Stranraer Museum. It is a pity that not more are available to show people today what their forefathers had to contend with in wresting a living from a dour land.

It is generally accepted that prior to the eighteenth century the Scots plough was the only cultivation instrument in use in that country. Nevertheless John Francis Erskine in his account of The State of Agriculture in Clackmanan county in 1795 states that by 1762 several ploughs were in use in Scotland, although of the incoming models Erskine makes the wry comment, 'There are a hundred different ploughs in England and all of them bad.' (14) One important factor in favour of the long-continued use of such a relatively fragile plough, apart from the inherent difficulties of its manufacture at that period, was the fact that only a limited area of the land was being cultivated. Lack of drainage was undoubtedly the main handicap although many other factors—political influence, landowning rules, population density, climate etc—all played a part. Regardless of the reasons the fact is that much of Scotland's most fertile land today was completely untouched in the early eighteenth century. At that time undrained areas provided very large grazing areas communally used around small ferm toun settlements: grain was for man; hay, which could be grown without cultivation on the outbye lands, was for animals.

Almost the whole of the Scots plough (Figure 3) was made of wood, only the sock and coulter being of iron; the head of the beam, the sheath, the wrest, even the mould board, the two handles and the two rungs were all of timber. The head of the plough, about $26 \times 5 \times 2\frac{1}{2}$ inches thick was rectangular, with the front six inches pointed. On one side it was morticed with two holes, one for the sheath and one for the handle, with the iron sock driven onto the pointed end. The sheath, driven into the front mortice was $13 \times 3 \times 1$ inches set at a backward angle of 60 degrees(14). 'The longer the head the steadier the plough' it was said; on the other hand the shorter it was, the more easily drawn. The head was made of alder but the mould board, still so called although of steel today, was then made of willow or even alder or plane, light and not too easily split. This crude implement made more of a triangular rut than a furrow,(15) but despite this it was quite capable, over centuries of use, of raising the broader rigs of that date into massses of soil 5 feet high and 200 yards long.

The Scots plough was a huge implement—13 feet from the handles to the beam and 4 feet from the back of the head to the point of the sock(24)—and although its power in uprooting boulders and tree roots proved its worth the friction of its movement was enormous. Its crudity and weight meant that it required a large team and several men to operate it and it was very difficult to turn. One plough was usually required for every 30 acres.(33) How it was used at any time and place was governed by a fascinating variety of factors, but over-shadowing them all was the fact that as time went on the Scots plough became obsolete and had to yield, unevenly but inexorably, in the various parts of the country, to the superior Small's plough, which will be described later.

The size and composition of the team required to manage the

3   The auld Scotch plough.

plough varied widely, but in the south of Scotland six cattle and
two horses were generally considered a full team; in the north ten
cattle, sometimes twelve (the 'twal owsen ploo') were yoked to
it.(15) This ensemble would be managed by a team of as many
as four men operating the yoke, together with the driver of the
team who walked backwards in front of his animals. Sometimes
instead of employing a gadsman walking alongside he was able
to make the horses come forward by striking them on the head
with a long whip or stick.(24)

   Both the choice and sometimes the mixture of animals was
dictated in some areas by proximity to adequate grazing land. In
Lowland parishes in summer all the oxen would be miles away
on the shielings with the sheep, tended by the younger women
and children. Stock simply could not be left at home to use up the
vital winter feed of hay and shrub growth. Some horses on the
other hand were required for the transport of men and goods and
had to be kept at home. That being so their use for other purposes
such as fallow ploughing was normal. Later in 1790 when horses
were likely to be bigger, better fed and stronger, two, three or
four farmers would join together in providing a plough team of
four or six horses to level old rigs and break in new ground.(24)

   Other factors also influenced the style of ploughing from place
to place. For example the Angus glens held on to the old plough
to the end of the century but the Angus lowlanders, loath to
adapt to the Small's plough, were fitting metal mould boards to

their old Scots ploughs rather than use the new all-metal models.(11) In the Glenshee area where, as in Breadalbane, horses were used as beasts of burden in preference to cattle, they yoked six horses in a row to pull the Scots plough, the driver again walking backward.(12) But the new field patterns and the new cultivation strategies also affected ploughing. In the first place the enclosed fields with their limited size and roughly rectangular shapes made the cumbrous Scots plough difficult to use in the old way and led in some cases to ploughing being done round and round from the circumference to the centre of the field or *vice versa*. This characteristic of the old plough had itself been a factor in the very long and narrow units of cultivation in earlier times. Lastly there was the fact that much of the cultivated landscape was being reploughed as the old steep-sided run-rigs were levelled. This was a somewhat easier task than before and could be handled by a less massive implement. In addition, on the new level arable ground the clods could be broken by rollers and a far better 'tilth' obtained for the sowing of grain.

No description of the Scots plough would be complete without reference to the 'riestle' (Figure 4). This was rather like a reaping hook, and on stiff land it was drawn through the soil about eight inches deep ahead of the plough. About three feet long and with a beam and one stilt but without a sock it could be worked by a single horse led by one man with another holding the stilt.(20) We can imagine the scene: first the riestle with two men and a horse, then a team varying from all the horses of the ferm toun, in line or even abreast, through a mixture of oxen and horses, to in some cases, twelve oxen, all with four men at the yoke. Slowly they would heave up the soil into long narrow mounds, first on one man's strip of land then on another's until all the rigs of the ferm toun were finished, and since each man possessed several strips of land many would be the hours spent in discussing the order of their cultivation. But the days of the Scots plough and this way of life were numbered, and in fact they did not survive the turn of the eighteenth century. The implement which shaped the land of Scotland was gone; the lands were level and the lads and lassies in their courting ploys were no longer safely hidden 'among the rigs o' barley-o'.

One exception to the universal use of the Scots plough, was the 'Highland Plough', referred to in Wight's *Husbandry* of 1773

4   The improved wooden plough.

(Figure 4). This primitive wooden tool was only 4 to 5 foot long and had only one stilt (handle) and a slight mould board fastened to it by two leather straps. The sock and coulter were bound together at the point with a ring of iron. Slight as it was it still required four horses yoked abreast to pull it. This tendency to yoke the animals abreast rather than in tandem suggests that those rigs would be shorter, and also that the tramping of the animals would flatten and break the clods, thus facilitating harrowing. For the latter operation, light wooden harrows often manually used, were necessary, wooden mallets also being used to break the clods. Not only was the heavy team required but three men were still essential to work it. The driver walked backwards in front with the reins fixed to a cross stick, while another walked by the side of the plough and a third followed with a spade. This plough was pulled by thongs or traces of leather.[20]

Small's plough

The great innovation in ploughing began in 1735 when James Small of Berwickshire introduced a much smaller plough, made largely of iron. Although it took 50 to 75 years to reach all of Scotland this plough was to revolutionise farming practice, altering the appearance of the whole countryside and causing a major diminution of the rural population. Known universally as Small's plough, it was a chain plough, very much shorter than the old models, far lighter and much more easily worked, and it could be drawn by two horses instead of the cumbersome yoke of up to twelve beasts. It could even be worked by one man, whereas up to four were required on the old plough. Although a boy might still be used to help the ploughman, the driver was no longer essential; one man between the stilts could not only steady and steer but also keep the animals moving. These efficient ploughs cost about one pound each and by 1770 were in general use in the Lowlands.[20]

The enormous advantages of the new plough opened up a new vista for the entrepreneur possessor keen to enlarge his holding and become a tenant farmer. Thus he ousted his old colleagues, leaving them to make their way to the towns, while he hired only the most able as his workers. A steady movement ensued of redundant men and their families away from rural areas as shown by the statistical accounts of this period. No trace of these people remains; their houses, insubstantial biggins of turf and stone, were ploughed over and buried; the stones were used for the new 'corn fences' which could be built now that this easily worked plough could turn so easily; and the divot and thatch of their construction used to fertilise the land. Along with this, of course, there were changes of a more positive nature; blacksmiths had to be trained and rural smithies set up in every parish, not only to make and service the new contraptions but also to shoe the horses and to furnish the carts which were now an essential part of farming life. (Farmers were often thirled to smithies as well as grain mills on the Laird's estate.)

The *Statistical Account* reports Small's plough in use as far north as Ardersier Parish around 1790. There it was termed the 'English plough' or, by the large farmers, 'Lord Kames' Plough'. Their status symbol was the new plough fitted with a chain, while their tenant farmers worked ploughs without such an embellishment! In Banffshire and Aberdeenshire other symbols appeared as the larger farmers began to vie with each other for ownership of the best team of ploughing oxen and clung with pride to their 'twal owsen ploo'. This was wasteful consumption pure and simple, for these heavy teams could plough only half an acre a day and there was much waste from foul threshing and stealing sheaves by these teams. The smaller farmers on the other hand, compelled to adopt the most efficient means possible, used Small's ploughs capable of being hauled by two horses and quite suitable in the gravelly soils.(15)

Under the impacts of all these developments, singly and in concert, the stage had been set for a radical change in the rural face of Scotland. Drainage had made more land available and usable, Small's plough had made it more amenable to cultivation, and marl and lime had made it more fruitful, all of them adding immeasurably to the economic vitality of the country, albeit at an immediate human cost. Dykes and tree planting had added pattern and texture to the landscape and started to temper the ferocity of the winds. Roads had made supplies of sporadically occurring materials such as marl and lime more widely available, facilitated commerce and aided the diffusion of crucial ideas and practices. In short, man had taken a bare, treeless land, underdeveloped yet abused, and set a much firmer imprint on it, one which, despite all the development of the last 200 years, we can recognise today as 'ours'.

6   THE LOWLAND CLEARANCES

The utilisation of land for profit led to a wholesale reduction in the number of people who earned their livelihood in country areas, and landowners who had formerly taken pride in the number of men on the clan land were now evicting them from what had become their personal estates. Nor, it seems, were many of them too sympathetic as they tended to 'shut up their bowels of mercy against the children of those who fell by their father's side'; 'The anguish and tears of their kindred had doubtful effect on melting their hearts'.(31) That the problems of displacement were not successfully dealt with was not due to lack of theories or proposals, for while this thinning out of the rural population was continuing and enclosure went on apace, some were claiming that all it required was more tillage, better agricultural management and more food production: 'There is a vast extent of arable ground at present under grass and which is daily increasing.'(30) Rodger claimed the lack of food and housing were causing emigration—'men are being forced off the land'—and advocated further enlargement and construction of villages in the rural areas to house the homeless. Others were less specific: 'There should be more humanity for making people happy and comfortable than in driving them from their native home'; 'Better to keep them at home as workers and artisans to provide an improved standard of life.'(31) Nor was some optimism unreasonable, for it had by now been proved that improved production off the now flat land could provide more food than under the run-rig techniques. Potatoes had been introduced and adequate land was still available for them; imported timber was coming in for house roofing and wooden floors; peat was in plentiful supply. Some who had previously farmed what they had considered their own land could be retained as paid land workers and it was hoped that the surplus would drift into the newly established villages and the enlarging towns. But the reality was different, one of the main difficulties being the expansion of sheep farming. This was far more rapid than expected so that the village system could not absorb the numbers displaced from the upland glens. In any event the absorption of land workers by the rapidly developing factories fell far behind the displacement of rural people, and while the strong went abroad the weak died off through hunger and want. 'Between the two rebellions (1715–45) the towns and villages doubled their population'; 'Some increased ten-fold while the agricultural population went down by a third';(31) and thousands were roaming the countryside, penniless, without any prospect of work.(31)

The problem of unemployment beset the whole of the eighteenth century. Andrew Fletcher of Saltoun claims that even in 1700 'about one fifth of the population were begging alms from door to door'. Even more, 'Many were dying yearly from absolute want.'(1) The Kirk session records of these early days confirm the large number of desperately poor people haunting the Kirk doors and bearing labels to distinguish licensed from unlicensed beggars. 'There were 100,000 gypsies or vaga-bonds.'(1) Many of these unemployed were not necessarily from the lower stratum of society; 'One half of the land properties of the Kingdom are possessed by a people who are all gentlemen only because they will not work'; 'They always carry arms because for the most part they live by robbery.'(1) The problem was still there as Fletcher wrote these lines well into the second half of the century, and he went so far as to advocate a form of slavery as a solution! Saying also that 'the Highlanders were an inexhaustible source which has always broken our measures to deal with them', he even suggested transposing Highlanders for Lowlanders!

In contemplating these conditions it is well to remember that at this time the law was quite ruthless, people being hanged for the theft of a horse or a cow. The days of inter-clan stock-lifting as a gentleman's pastime were over and relatively minor offenders were being transported abroad as felons. Prisons as known today were largely in the future although the ideas of workinghouses or bridewells as an alternative were developing. It was considered that solitary confinement and hard labour would be a general deterrent and more to be feared than the gibbet, which was at that time the law's answer to relatively minor crimes often committed in desperation by a starving and disillusioned people. However the cost of shipping large numbers of prisoners abroad was beginning to be quite significant and the construction and management of prisons with some return from forced labour was thought to be an interesting alternative.

Rural industries

A product of these same times—presumably arising, among other things, from the increased production of the countryside and the presence of cheap and docile labour—was rural industry. Generally rural industry tended to spring up at the place of origin of its basic materials, for transport on land was extremely difficult. Thus the early iron-smelting works, utilising wood fuel, were naturally near the remnants of the original climax-vegetation woods, which were quickly denuded. It was cheaper to transport iron ore from the Midlands to the northwest forests and the resultant product south again than to move the wood, even by sea, to the source of iron. This was not, of course, the source of all industrial development, for many of the very early industries in the small towns of Scotland had their origins south of the border. As an instance 'the tanning of leather and the making of shoes were introduced into Inverness-shire by the soldiers of Cromwell'(14) and much of the trade in Scotland must have flowed from the English garrisons and from ideas brought north with the soldiers. In addition, as time went on and industries expanded in scale, some activities, notably weaving, spinning and related processes, tended to settle on streams which could yield water-power for their mills. And of course nothing stood still. New processes and larger and more efficient machines always had both positive and negative effects, new jobs being created while others were made obsolete.

Thus the people of Crieff, who for long depended on the passage of cattle from the north and of goods to and from the Highlands, came to tan leather and make a coarse paper. They also started a tambour school to teach young girls spinning and a linen manufactory, soon to outstrip the old handlooms and deprive the rock-and-spindle hand spinners of Loch Tay and Kenmore of their livelihood and drive them to the mills and bleachfields near Perth.

Hand knitting of woollen garments on a commercial scale for export became an important rural industry in the Aberdeen area. Towards the end of the century huge numbers of home-knitted woollen stockings, mainly for army use, left the port from the surrounding countryside.(33) While most of the early hand-woven linen goods were made in the towns a surprising amount were made far inland and carried to market on the weaver's back or by horse. By 1790 Doune township had deserted pistol-making and in exploiting the new cotton fibre had utilised the ample water supply of the River Teith to power a cotton mill.

A more detailed example of rural industry is afforded by Barry Parish which by 1780 was exporting locally woven brown linen. Prior to this much of the linen thread used by early weaving factories in Glasgow was hand spun in the glens and rural parts of Perth and Angus and bought up there by intermediate merchants at periodic fairs. Wool spinning and weaving had preceded flax and linen and early in 1700 the second Earl of Breadalbane had brought wool workers from England to teach spinning and weaving on Loch Tayside. Flax was first raised on the spade-dug and turf-walled tofts of the run-rig crofts in 1728.(36) Six years later the tenants were selling lint yarn at the Kenmore markets, hand-spun by spindle and distaff on the braes along Loch Tay, and soon £1,600 worth of this home-spun thread was sold at the four markets held at Kenmore each year.(31) With the advent of spinning wheels the third Earl was trying to encourage the trade by giving away a number of wheels each year. By 1770 the Lawers lint mill dressed 460 stones of flax and Killin 954 stones,(36) the flax being 'scutched' by separating the fibres by water-driven mechanisms, the first scutching mills in the Highlands. By 1793 Kenmore village was a thriving little town with 63 weavers, 38 tailors, 36 wrights, 26 shoemakers, 20 flax dressers, 10 smiths, 9 masons, 8 coopers, 4 hosiers and a dyer,(36) a total of over 200 artisans in the area. Most of these workers came from the Lochside crofts then being amalgamated and cleared. However there were still 555 small farmers, 207 crofts and 69 cottars on the ground.(36) At the north end of the

Loch, Killin was also drawing in land workers to become artisan producers. It housed 36 weavers, 22 tailors, 14 wrights, 10 shoemakers, 6 smiths, 7 merchants and 2 bakers. The land-working weaver soon died out when water-powered machines replaced his leg muscles on the loom treadle. Lord Kames tells us that his contemporaries were advocating 'that the weaver should now devote his time to his trade and that he should sever his age-old link with the land and give up his old run-rig holding'. The noble Lord, however, was of the opinion that he was better to retain the land, 'since its possession and the improved health caused by having to work' on it 'gave the weaver a balance of several extra years of work caused by the health-giving exercise'. 'In any case the weaver only required four acres of land, as he did not need a horse'.(24) A difficulty of that time (1790) was that there 'was seldom a market in Scotland where he could buy provisions even if his trade earned him enough money to buy food rather than raise it himself'.(24) By this time many mills were in operation: Bridge of Allan had a bleach mill driven by its fast-running river while the Almond near Perth was harnessed to power a chain of mills. To these mills flocked the surplus agricultural population, soon to realise that they had deserted agricultural poverty in the open air for a worse fate in an enclosed mill.

Along with these developments went the growth of towns and villages, for in the early part of the eighteenth century the vast majority of the population lived in the countryside. Route crossings and harbours gathered a sprinkling of merchants and tradesmen with their followers, but until the advent of specialised manufacturing there was little necessity for many of the towns that quickly sprang up in the nineteenth century. In earlier times some families chose the relative shelter of living near the castle of a Baron while many of today's small towns owe their existence to the sanctuary of a nearby abbey. Nevertheless many of our apparently old towns have quite short histories; Callander for instance, with a population of 1,000 in 1794, held only about four families in 1730.(31)

In the early years of the century even the principal towns each held a small population leading the life of a large village. There would be a large proportion of the well-to-do and their servants, and the rural lairds had town houses or lodgings. A large number of the inhabitants who no longer needed to grow their own oatmeal still managed to keep a cow by grazing it on the open land near the town. They also kept a pig or two within the burgh wall and there was usually swill available from the establishments of the gentry. Cultivators also had ample night soil available from the dry closets then in use, for water-carriage of sewage had to await the development of fireclay piping. Thus some of the nearby land could maintain a heavy crop of greens, but often much of the land close to the town was still grassland and heath and quite unenclosed. Without police or adequate fencing, crop production was a hazardous business and even in the countryside the high walls round the gardens of the rich were built to exclude pilferers as much as to grow wall-fruit trees.

By the last quarter of the century prominent landowners were looking for sites for new towns and villages to absorb the people they were decanting off their estates. In addition many sought to profit from the sale and feu of land. This formation of new villages relied more on the enterprise of the local landowner than of the potential villagers or the entrepreneur manufacturer. In fact the Laird, desiring status from village ownership and income from the feuing of land, usually had to seek out and tempt the skilled machine-maker to his area by promise of water power or ample cheap labour. Thus 'Mr Drummond of Comrie has lately laid out the village of Dalginross and a market place on a completely barren moor covered with a thin moss and a bed of gravel.' 'The new settlers are laying a new soil and improving the ground.' (30)

Thus also after George Dempster the local landowner near Forfar engaged a surveyor to lay out a new town at Letham, Angus in 1788, 'Streets were laid out, the new houses built of stone and lime, two stories high and all slated.' (12) This was in direct contrast to the primitive turf-and-stone, scattered biggins with thatched roofs from which the new feuars came. Some 200 of these families soon moved into his new town, paying him £2 per acre in perpetual feu. They were by then comparatively well off, for most of the women were hand-spinning flax fibre into linen thread and wool for their men folks, who were busy weaving on hand-looms in the new houses. The bi-annual or quarterly fairs for the selling of thread, yarn and cloth were now superseded by a fortnightly market, when some £500 would change hands. The cloth was by then manufactured in Letham whereas in earlier days only the thread had been locally produced and then exported. Not only were progressive landowners aided to a large extent by the Commissioners of the Forfeited Estates, but the Commissioners themselves were using their powers to create new communities out of the rural wreckage in the aftermath of the 1745 rebellion. 'In 1763, the villages of Callander, Comrie (later to be enlarged by the adjacent Dalginross across the river), Muthill, Methven and Longforgan were "built" by the commissioners.' (30)

The older towns and settlements had grown naturally beside water sources and built up the network of roads serving them, these roads then being an invitation to further growth. Later of course the nearby river tended to become a source of town wealth by its power-creating ability. The new towns, on the other hand, strategically situated from some viewpoints but sadly deficient from others, often had their problems. Take for example 'Auchterarder then a pleasant town but quite without water in summer, except a spring about a quarter mile to the north and on low ground'. 'In winter and spring a small ditch carries water from the high ground along the side of the street to each house.'(35) Even the more fortunate communities created both by natural growth and the will of administrators had problems of water supply and, later, drainage. Many solved the problem by diverting a nearby stream to flow along the village street, as at Muthill, where at a much later date the villagers, tired of the stench of such a diverted stream, took advantage of legislation designed to provide piped drainage. They formed themselves into a properly rated Drainage District whose sole sewage works consisted of a stout broom which the drainage officer used to sweep the bed of the diverted stream!

A distinctive group were those with a foot both in the village and in the country, early farmers who had not yet acquired enough land or managerial skill to make a profit and an independent living away from their lands. Also, 'The early farmers were reckoned to need a trade as well as farm work.'(19) As the surplus peasantry flocked into the towns unions evolved to protect earlier won trade rights against their competition. To become a 'freeman' of a trade union involved serving a seven-year apprenticeship or paying a heavy fee. So the rural farmer-tradesmen could not move readily to a town nor could they be employed as town tradesmen since they were not freemen.(19) However a more persistent farmer, a would-be joiner perhaps, would seek out one of the more easy-going corporations, such as the Bowers or Fletchers, who tried to profit by admitting new members at a reduced fee. Once accepted by them as a freeman, although they had no connection with his trade as a joiner, he was free to set up as a craftsman in the town. The only thing the more principled corporations could do was to restrict his voting rights to his new Union, not allowing him to vote with the joiners! The transforming of the farmer into a town dweller was only one side of the picture. On the other hand it was also recognised as a fact of life 'that a tradesman required sufficient land to grow food for his own family'.(24) These independent Wrights and Weavers, Masons and Smiths etc required at least six acres to keep their horse for transport and a cow for milk. Thus they tended to group themselves within walking distance of a town or village in order to ply their trade there yet still farm at home, and it was quite normal for them to walk five or more miles each day to their work to be there at normal starting time. As a result small tradesmen's crofts and holdings were often found near towns and villages.

7 DAY TO DAY LIVING

Work and wages

Wages and salaries in the transition period between open run-rig and enclosed flat cultivation were remarkably stable. Lord Kames quotes day wages before 1770 at 8*d*. per day for a man and 1*s*.2*d*. per day for a horse! By 1775 Wight quotes 10*d*. per day as wages in the Stobhall area in Perthshire. In Angus two years later Rodger considered that farm workers were too highly paid at 1*s*.2*d*. per day without board or 10*d*. per day with board. The practice, however, was to pay men only for the eight working months of the year from before seed time to after harvest. With so much labour available from the people displaced off the run-rigs there was no real need for work on the land during the winter or in the summer growing season; casual labour could be had in abundance at any time for 1*s*. per day. Those engaged annually could command, for a full year's work £7, £10 and £12 per annum according to their age and ability. This would work out at well under 1*d*. per hour but on this basis they were fed, by the farmer, albeit on very plain and monotonous food. Near the end of the agricultural transition period—about 1790—the *Statistical Account* confirms a wage in Monikie Parish still at £7–10 per annum plus meals. As a comparison, at that time the minister could command a salary of £115 per annum and the schoolmaster about £35. The change over from the run-rigs was thus carried out very cheaply but with extreme hardship to the lower classes.

Married men with families would receive two pecks of meal a week, a Scots pint of milk daily and some salt occasionally, all this being valued at 1*s*. per week. The single men lived together in a bothy feeding almost exclusively on a diet of oatmeal brose. These men would rise at 5 a.m. to dress and feed the horses and muck out the stable. At 6.30 a.m. they would have their morning brose in the bothy, starting work at 7 a.m. Some demanding grieves (farm stewards) started their men even earlier, the starting time being at the field, no matter how distant, yoked and ready to begin and not at the steading or stable! After working for four hours without a break the horses required a rest—they were more important than the workers—and they were unyoked about noon and stabled, to be fed at 1 p.m. Meantime the men carried out various manual jobs and took their second brose meal before 2 p.m. After another four hours field labour the horses were again stabled and fed after 6 p.m. The men could then have their third brose meal of the day in the bothy. During the summer they worked from 4 a.m. to 9 p.m.(12)

Food

Following the failure of the grain crops in the period from 1695 to 1702 there was extreme poverty at the beginning of the eighteenth century. As already indicated Andrew Fletcher of Saltoun states 'about one fifth of the population in 1700 were begging from door to door'. For the landless and jobless poor the Laird's castle and the Kirk Session afforded the only relief available. In earlier times the Catholic churches in particular had acted as store houses in good times and dispensaries in dearth, and although it may well be true that the monks lived on the best of everything the 'crumbs that fell' prevented starvation for many. With the Reformation in 1560 the abbeys and monasteries disappeared but their stock-piled granaries were not replaced by the Presbyterian regime despite the irony that jealousy for the wealth and good living of the Catholic Church may well have helped to bring about the Reformation.

One factor contributing to this poverty was the almost complete dependence on what little grain could be grown and harvested, eked out by such animal food as was available, particularly fish, shellfish, milk and blood. The growing of vegetables was little practised by the general public apart from some seasonal kale and parsnips; peas were grown but mainly as a field crop for use as grain; turnips and potatoes had still to be introduced. Educated landowners were trying, by example and publicity, to increase vegetable production, but while they could protect their gardens by high walls the tenants—unless they built small stone-walled enclosures, the 'planty cribs' of the Highlands—were unable to overwinter anything since from September to May everything edible would be eaten by their neighbours' stock, this being the established custom of the times. Thus when Locheil of Achnacarry in Lochaber, having relished the fresh vegetables he found abroad, established a kitchen garden in 1734, he was able to feed his guests a vegetable stew of peas, carrots and turnips—the first time they had ever tasted such food, as vegetables were not grown in the Highlands at all. In the Lowlands too John Walker DD of Edinburgh states that in his time only the big houses had gardens, while in Central Scotland Lord Kames was strongly advocating the growing of vegetables—as a means of reducing the cost of keeping staff, for up to 1760 servants were fed almost exclusively on oatmeal! Near the east and west coasts fish were a welcome source of food, the seasonal herring shoals being so plentiful as to be virtually unsaleable. Unfortunately they could not readily be preserved owing to lack of salt which, being heavily taxed was scarce and expensive. Casks also were difficult to make or come by, which inhibited transport of this rich source of protein to less favoured areas.

Bad harvests could put back the dietary clock and around 1773 after meagre harvests the universal diet in rural areas was miserably poor. The food was 'bere' (primitive barley) meal porridge morning and evening; the midday meal was the same, possibly with a few boiled greens to eke out the meal. In that year oats were almost impossible to obtain and only a few had some dried peas to mix with their 'bere' meal.(35) Soon even barley meal for porridge became unobtainable and recourse was had to 'mealy kail', a poor broth with a little meal to give it substance. Potatoes were coming into use however, and soon became a universal food.

Home life was crude in the first half of the eighteenth century. Tables in rural homes were virtually non-existent, and the ordinary farmer, even as late as 1780, ate his food not at a table but out of a wooden bowl or brose cap resting on his knee.(31) Meal, some kale and milk were the monotonous rule, morning, noon and night. He lay at night on a bed of chaff, heather or straw on the ground, for there were as yet no wood floors in ordinary dwellings. By 1795 however, the surviving farmer rode to market, ate off a table covered with a cloth, used a knife and fork and even had meat to eat with some regularity. By this time also he slept on a feather-filled mattress with curtains drawn round his elevated wooden bed, though in many cases the floor, certainly of the lower apartments, was still of beaten clay or stone flags. Such progress of course varied very much from district to district.

By this date also our emerging farmer could afford fresh meat, which could even be obtained all the year round owing to better pasturage and winter feed whereas around 1740 only salt beef was obtainable after Martinmas. Butter and cheese were readily available in certain areas such as Aberdeenshire, where almost all the milk available was so used. The residual whey was kept to augment the greens and potatoes then used to supplement oatmeal. Even the milk which was sent to Aberdeen for sale as such was first creamed of its fat for butter.(33) Oatmeal was generally scarce, the demands of the populace exceeding production, and this combined with bad harvests pushed the change towards more vegetables and potatoes. Although by this time goods were more plentiful the ordinary labourer employed on day wages had a thin time of it. In good years his wage of possibly 10d. per day would buy one $\frac{1}{4}$ pecks of oatmeal or $\frac{3}{4}$ peck of barley meal but not 4 lb of mutton or beef. Meat was 3d. to 4d. per lb; 24 ounces of cheese was 2d. to 3d., and butter 6d. to 9d. A dozen eggs cost 2d. to 3d., which could also buy a chicken. Hens however were 6d. to 8d., a duck 7d. to 9d. and a goose 2s. to 2s.6d.(15) It was only on Sundays and Christmas holidays that meat or fish were seen on workers' tables; otherwise a diet of oatmeal and potatoes was universal.(15)

In the eighteenth century bread as we know it today is seldom mentioned, for while wheat bread was being used in England it was still unknown in rural Scotland where people were largely dependent on oatmeal bannocks. In an endeavour to produce some variety in this monotonous diet some used the wasteful 'graddan' bread, produced by burning the whole of the top part of the sheaf and grinding the scorched grain into flour. This practice, which deprived the land of humus, was deliberately banned in some farm leases.

As an interesting sidelight it appears that while in England a family required a third of an acre of wheat to survive, in Scotland it required an acre of oats and in Ireland $\frac{1}{4}$ acre of potatoes. In England the labourer was reckoned to need 107–110 bushels of wheat per year for his family of five at a time when his wages only brought in three-quarters of this. The farming landowners there contrived to get the balance met by Church poor funds!(14)

Not unrelated to food is the topic of whisky. Although brewing had been much more popular at an earlier date, at the start of the century a dominant feature of the glens and rural areas was the distillation of whisky. This of course consumed a large proportion of the barley grown on the old run-rigs. Wight reports 'all the barley in Stobhall went to the glens for whisky and not to Perth' for sale to the townsfolk. Towards the end of the eighteenth century whisky was so plentiful that an English pint in an ale house cost only 4d., but even at this price it would still cost the equivalent of a day's manual toil! Much ingenuity and energy were expended in the traffic of this illicit product, as in the smuggling of other taxable goods, and agriculture suffered as a result. Even well into the nineteenth century farms along the sea coast were often poor and neglected since they were used largely as an excuse to maintain horses whose main purpose was to carry inland smuggled goods landed from the sea.(13)

Fuel

The eighteenth century was a period of crisis in the use of fuel. Whatever damage may have been done to the original forests by deliberate burning to eliminate wolves or people, in 1700 there were still enough trees for the needs of the relatively small number of country dwellers. But the century witnessed a steady reduction of that supply.

We must not underestimate the use of twigs and brushwood as fuel in the small stone-and-turf hovels of the poorer classes. The windowless hut with a low door and a cow for company and heat did not require a large fire to maintain sufficient warmth. Since peat and divot were difficult to cut, carry and dry, the ample supply of children—with no schooling to occupy their day— would scour the countryside for every dead twig or branch, for these were adequate to heat the midday pot of kale, and of course there was no teapot to require hot water. The occasional washing of clothes was done outside on dry days and twigs would also suffice for that purpose. The luxury of the everlasting fire may have been sustainable in areas with ample peat near at hand but could not have been universal. Just as the poor in India and China today carry bundles of twigs for long distances so must our foremothers have performed similar duties only two hundred years ago.

While every sizeable tree had already been felled and little or no planting carried out, there was still some scrub of alder and birch, particularly in the 'riske' or boggy areas abounding in a drainless land. In addition broom was sown and planted on the south-facing foothills of the Sidlaw hills for eventual use as fuel. The reason for this is given by the local minister in the *Statistical Account*: 'The roads were quite impractical for loaded carts in the winter season'; 'They made practical the sowing of broom for fuel because the cost of carrying coal was so heavy'.(33) In the reed-covered Carse of Gowrie the early roads, such as they were, ran mainly from the hill villages of the Sidlaws to the River Tay, not east to west as they do today. There was little trade between Perth and Dundee and what there was went more easily by boat or on pack horses.

General use of coal came later when better roads were available, although from an early date it was carried to landowners' castles on horseback in panniers. It was also available early on by boat at the many coastal landing places, either off a pier or by beaching the boat at high tide. We know from Inglis(25) that for the burning of a witch in Forfar 'John Millar paid £3.6.8. for 10 loads of coal, 14s for a tar barrel and 6s for towes'. The weavers of Forfar could not have used so costly a fuel in their household grates.

As the wood supply dried up, divots and peat were about the only fuel along with the fir and birch limbs buried in the bogs. Soon the heritors adjoining the mosses, observing their diminution, were endeavouring to control their usage. Recourse was always made to burning divot, the top spit of soil from uncultivated land, a dreadful practice which consumed the good soil on the slopes of most of the Lowland hills. In this shallow top spit thousands of years of grass roots had accumulated, fertilised in time by the action of worm castings, with not a stone or a grain of sand buried in it. Where it still remained on lowland and upland pastures which had never been cultivated it was now stripped off without thought for the loss of fertility and either burned in the ferm toun houses or even carried off to be burned on a worked-out piece of outfield in process of enclosure and improvement. The gross wastage of this magnificently fertile soil base by burning was akin to the twentieth-century wasteful flaring off of 'surplus' gas from oil wells. So scarce was wood and peat and so expensive was coal that when ground was being feued off for merchants' houses in the older towns the feuar's lawyers insisted that the landowner, who also owned land on nearby hillsides, write into the charter the right of the feuar to strip divot from the hillside lands. Very small patches of this natural material still may exist even near large towns, while in an isolated glen in Aberdeenshire I met one farmer in 1970 who still stripped and dried the hillside turf for his winter fuel (Figure 5), volunteering that divot, when dried out, made good though rather dusty fuel. As this was more easily obtained than peat the bulk of the hills near habitations were stripped early in the eighteenth century, and by mid century the more accessible peat deposits were also being depleted: 'By this time (1755) in the Parish of Rattray the mosses were mostly exhausted and coals were expensive.'(33) Also in Udny Parish in Aberdeenshire 'Peats and turf are getting scarce and the sub-tenants are moving from the Parish to the neighbouring parishes'(33) (the sub-tenants being the mobile element of the population, the first to move away from a situation that was no longer viable). Those remaining in the area—for the rural population was already shrinking—took steps to safeguard their rights against new-comers and not only was turf-stripping restricted on privately owned hillsides but the commons also were often protected: 'Auchterarder Burgh muir was available to Burgers only, for feal or divot cutting.'(35)

Peat bogs were being cut not only by individuals for their own use but also commercially. Incidentally a 'drag' or 'dargue' of peat, used as a measure, was the amount one man could cut and two could wheel to the field where they were to dry, this amount varying according to circumstances at the bog. Centuries later the 'day's dargue' remains a colloquial term for a normal day's

5   A 1970 load of grass divot, still used as fuel.

work. The *Statistical Account* of 1790 recounts many tales of the stripping of hillside pastures for fuel: 'The hills to the south east of Kirkhill Parish were pretty high and were covered with heath. The pasture was miserably poor since the surface was constantly carried off for burning as fuel.'(33) The fuel situation was not relieved by the duty on coal at the pithead. From Kells and Berwick Parishes comes the cry: 'Again and again protests were made about the duty on coals and the need to spend all summer getting poor turf from 8 to 10 miles away.' From Aberdeenshire in 1790 comes the same complaint: 'By 1790 there were no peats to be had'; 'Fuel was generally turf and heather from the hill'; 'Wood was finished years ago' and coal was just coming in. 'In the parish of Udny it took most of the summer to cut, dry and cart the turf and the peats.'(33) Both fuels were being used and both were near exhaustion point.

Tallow

As candles were the main source of light in the houses of the eighteenth century, tallow, fat and oil were in great demand. Fat or oil of any kind would provide light in the metal cruisies (lamps) but for a candle it was then necessary to have intestinal suet. 'The main object in fattening sheep and cattle was to get the maximum amount of fat and tallow, which was worth more than the meat.'(24) Even as late as 1775 tallow sold for 5s.4d. per stone against 4s. for meat. All the sheep and cattle were thus kept to a ripe old age to provide the maximum tallow, to the extent that for the last year of their lives they were force fed.(24) Butchers with a dual product from their trade were thriving. 'The butcher's profit was considered to be not less than 5% of the cost of the beast in the market.'(24)

At an earlier date the small, windowless houses of the common man had little need for light for they could only have been night-time sleeping shelters, and a splinter of bog fir lit from the smokey embers would be their only illumination. With better houses and evening spinning and weaving a candle became a necessity, and the early spinning and weaving factories were all lit by candles. Some of the water wheels powered grain mills by night since these could be worked in the dark, while cloth production or

finishing powered by the same water wheel was carried out
during the day to save the expense of candles. This was salvation
for the women and children so employed who would otherwise
have been worked night and day like slaves, for in these days
labour was considered a capital asset to be utilised regardless of
the workers' needs.

Houses

While the castles, abbeys, churches and many burgh houses were
well built masonry structures, often with good joinery detail,
there is no doubt that at the start of the eighteenth century the
rural peasantry housed themselves in extremely primitive
fashion. The lack of timber, which became more and more acute
as the century progressed, turned the common man to construct
his hovels of rough boulders and turf with primitive covering of
branches and divot more often than thatch on the roof. At that
period however the divot, the top layer of grass sod, was a
substantial, well-knit material. Large patches a yard broad
could be cut with a knife or spade and made to lie securely on the
rough timber of the roof, and although it would admit drips it
would knit together and shed most of the rain. A dry summer,
killing the growing grass on the roof, would cause more harm to
such a roof than any winter storm.

Comparatively little is known of the pre-1700 houses of the
peasantry of Scotland and virtually no example exists today.
Where suitable stone was readily available and where later
housebuilders did not rob the ruins for their own purposes, some
remains of early dwellings are still visible, but only in ruins which
barely indicate the shape of the dwelling. Little comment was
made in contemporary writings of the detail of workers' housing
in the town areas.

The lack of permanence in the houses of the rural land dwellers
is apparent in Pennant's description of life south of Loch
Tay:(28) 'The houses of the Highlanders are in small groups:
they are very small, mean and without windows or chimneys.'
'They are a disgrace to north Britain.'(11) Wright confirms this
in his description of conditions between Perth and Coupar
Angus. There it would seem that the houses, built with sod roofs

and turf walls, only served a few years and periodically the whole house was demolished and spread out as manure. He also confirms the absence of windows or chimneys at that time (1769). And again, 'The tenants' houses on the Perth estates are little better than graves above ground built of sods and the best soil off the fields.'(35) In the Dunkeld area the thatch was of broom 'which lasts 3 or 4 years'. Erskine, writing reminiscently late in the century in *The General View of Agriculture* says bluntly, 'In former days the houses were miserable hovels.'

It is striking to contrast these sod houses of Scotland with the strong, substantial wooden houses then being built by rural dwellers in Norway. Although the fireplace and sleeping platforms were equally primitive, the walls were of solid logs, some still existing today. The roofs, insulated by large sheets of birch bark, were quite waterproof, and though similarly sod-covered they were dry and lasted a generation or more. These dwellings, which of course reflected the dense forests of Norway, were palaces compared to Scottish hovels of the time.

For the primitive possessor of the run-rig strips the house was basically a sleeping shelter in which he could sit beside his smouldering fire during the cold dark months, the warmth being provided mainly by the cattle which shared the single room of his dwelling. How this changed during his boyhood in Angus is described by Headrick of Dunnichen(18), 'The smoke-hole in the roof let in light; when greater light was required the door was opened.' The first improvement was a screen at the door to keep the draught off those round the fire. This was termed a 'hallen'. 'Later came a window in the wall and lastly a pane of glass', and still later we have a proper window with from one to three panes. 'Then "box beds" formed an internal division and later the but-and-ben was contrived, the farmer and his wife in the ben and the servants in the but end.' 'By that time a fireplace had been contrived in the ben end.' 'Wrought clay was then substituted for turf in the walls' and 'eventually lime pointing or harling became possible after the formation of roads and access to lime'.(12)

Home-grown fir timber was very scarce and Erskine, speaking of Muckhart, tells us that foreign timber was unavailable there until 1780.

Anderson of Aberdeen, commenting that in his day the houses of the rural dwellers were much improved, says, 'The landlord

6   The roof timber, made of old portions of wood branches.

was providing the timber for the erection of the new tenant houses. The lease stipulated however that an equal value of growing timber must be left at the end of the lease.'(13) This stimulated more tree planting, not necessarily of conifers, for the main trusses of the roof would still be hazel, birch, ash or oak limbs in short lengths pinned together (Figure 6) and rising from practically ground level with walling interfill. In the upland areas of Aberdeenshire these houses were now being thatched with heather, requiring sawn timbers. A net of ropes secured the whole roof surface. Says Anderson, 'They are seldom watertight and need constant repair.'(13)

The change in house construction and its relationship to economic improvement are best summarised in the *Statistical Account* with reference to Moneydie Parish: 'The lower farmers who up to the 1790's had been used to build their own stone and divot houses, began to employ masons to build them of stone and mortar, harling them on the outside with lime and then thatch them with straw and clay.'(33) Rodger of Angus (1794) was also saying 'Farmhouses are fast improving and are being built of two storeys with slated roofs.'(12) The houses of the major landowners were steadily improving long before that, and by the third quarter of the century the use of quarried stone with its expensive transport, hitherto reserved for the houses of the wealthy, was now being used for the better farmers' dwellings and offices.

Generally, of course, the character of the dwellings depended largely on the availability of materials. In the west, 'They erected creel houses where wood was to be had, of post interlaced with branches and covered with turf' (20), this being written at a time when, according to Wight, 'Most of the farms in the Muthill area are now building or have built houses with offices.'(35) The scarcity of some materials such as nails in certain areas is interesting: 'The early slating in the Highlands (up to 1800) was held together by heather roots'(27) and even in 1850 'A man going to Inverness on some great occasion would bring back enough nails with him to fix his coffin when the time came.'(27)

Deeper insight into both the buildings and the way of life in these times is afforded by comments and records on several larger buildings. The session records of Kenmore Parish tell of the erection of the school house there in 1751: 'It was still however built with dry unmortared stone, walls "roofed with cabers" and "covered with thatch with dore and bands".' This original use of the word caber is interesting. Now confined to the Highland games arena, it is here used in its original meaning of the roof timbers of a house. These cabers, doubtless the main wooden-dowelled cruick trusses, 'were obtained from the birch and hazel trees of "Coille Tom Nan Ceap"' (the wood of the sod mound) near Kenmore.(36)

The contemporary comment on the erection of the first hostelry at Kenmore ferry, built by Sir Colin Campbell in 1752, confirms the rarity of elementary items in buildings of the period: 'This house had chimneys, doors and windows!'(36) (To ensure that a suitable tenant would always carry on the business in this marvel of modernity, Sir Colin Campbell stipulated in the lease that should mine host die the widow could only take a new spouse of his Lordship's approval!) The scarcity of timber is confirmed in that the roofless church at Lawers, a not uncommon situation having regard to the type of roof material, was re-roofed in 1760 with native Scots pine wood from the Black Wood of Rannoch.

Most of the old castles were similarly roofed with timber from the then apparently inexhaustible Caledonian Forest.

Killin Session records provide a detailed account of the building of Killin Church in 1744, in which the work and materials would have been much better than those of normal houses. The new Church, which cost £3,120 Scots, was built by a Thomas Scott, and although he left only details of his extra items to the main contract these are interesting. The benefit of using the recently imported seasoned Baltic deals for the large window sashes was appreciated and these were acquired although this, compared with the use of native Scots Fir still available from Rannoch, added more than 6 per cent to the cost of the building. Slaters, an unknown craft locally, were brought in from the south to roof the church, the first slated building for miles around. Unlike tradesmen of a much later date who were paid only for the days they worked or even, in intermittent heavy rain, for the actual number of hours spent actively working, the Killin slaters were treated like estate retainers, retained for his Lordship's service as and when required, regardless of hours worked or the time of day or night called upon. When the employing family moved to the capital or to England for long periods the household servants who did not accompany them had little to do and they were then paid 'board wages' until the master's return a sum sufficient to maintain life but far less than a normal wage. Here at Killin the slaters were paid 'board wages' in bad weather—a legitimate extra on Thomas Scott's contract price! Other extras were for a plumber working on the erection of the bell and a painter gilding it. 'A glob for the cupola' was also an extra, this being brought by boat and off-loaded at Alloa. Since it took some time for news of its arrival to reach Killin, £2 was paid for its safe custody at Alloa (this was termed 'cellar rent') and £2.10s. was charged for 'express to Alloa to know if the glob for the cupola had come'.

Donald Sage's account of the erection of the manse at Loch Carron in 1729 also gives an insight into the life of the better classes in those times. This manse was 100 feet long of stone with walls 3 foot high all round. The wood-framed cruik roof trusses were carried to the ground and built into these low walls. The remainder of the walls were then built up with turf and divot a further 10 to 15 feet. This divot or feal was substantial enough for walling even for better class dwellings. The trusses were exposed in this upper section and branches were then carefully cross-laid on the trusses. The roof was carried clear over the walls at the eaves and thatched with long stems of old heather from the hill. One end of the building was occupied by 'the chamber', which had a chimney in the end gable and a glazed window. The wood partition which divided it from the next room contained within it a 'tent bed', known in the east as a box bed, which was fully enclosed to ensure privacy and was reserved for special guests. Next came a room where the heads of the family sat and had their meals; off it were tent beds for the junior members of the family and an access to the chamber. Third came a compartment opening off the second where the Minister and his wife slept. These three rooms comprised the private apartment of the Minister.

Next there was the large 'cearn' or servant's hall which had a fireplace in the centre of the room with a wicker 'hanging lum' guiding the smoke out through a hole in the roof. The hearth was an old millstone. The cearn was lit by small, unglazed, boarded windows in both outer walls, which were closed on the windward side when necessary and opened on the lee side to light the room. The cearn opened off the common lobby and from it a door entered the byre, comprising half the length of the building, which had stalls for milk cows next the hall and a court for loose cattle in the far gable. The staff slept in the loft space above the cattle, with hay stored in the far end. The heat from the animals would permeate the long roof space and help to heat the whole building.

8 RELIGION

Throughout the eighteenth century religion played a dominant role in the life of Scotland, all the more because of the schism between the Presbyterian and Episcopalian churches which persisted following the Reformation. This schism divided families, communities and parishes and affected both town and country, the latter probably more than the former because of rural affiliations with clans and landowning families, which were seldom neutral in the great power struggles of that time. Agriculture was affected directly, for in the early days the farm lands of the abbeys and their granges had probably been more important in promoting agriculture and horticulture than had the large landowners, who were more concerned with inter-clan warfare. In this respect the Catholic faith was probably more progressive than its successor Protestantism, for the latter was superstitious, doctrinaire and intolerant. For example the introduction of a man-driven winnowing device for removing the chaff from the corn grains was restricted by the narrow-minded as an unholy use of the 'Devils wind'. And both Church and estates levied substantial tithes on the land worker.

In the upheaval of the Reformation an enormous part of Scotland's visible history was ruthlessly burnt and much of what little civilisation existed in a crude and rebellious land died in the ashes of the abbeys and cathedrals. In the turmoil the lairds saw their chance, grabbed as much of the countryside as they could and maintained their authority through the Baron's courts. After several somersaults of fortune however, the Protestant faith became dominant and maintained its sway throughout the eighteenth century. As the years went on the church became fragmented into innumerable sects—the Free Church, the Wee Frees, the Burgers and the Anti-burgers, the Seceders, the Lifters and the Anti-lifters and more. Thus in a single parish with a village of less than fifty families there would often be four different churches, each proclaiming a different way of worshipping the same God, not to mention a few dissenters who would travel outside the parish to worship in Catholic or Episcopal chapels. In spite of this disputatious spirit and lack of unity, during the eighteenth century the church was the main force for stability in a still turbulent society, acting as both religious and civil authority.

The early rural churches were humble affairs, most having earth floors and thatch roofs. They would have a sturdy pulpit, a daske or fixed seat for the elders and later, pews for the laird and the larger heritors. The members of the congregation had to take their own 'creepie' stools to attend the service. The possession of a Bible and a Psalm Book was essential for every house and these had to be marked with 'their ane name'.

The governance of the churches was undertaken by the Kirk Sessions, composed of the owners of heritable property with the notable exception in many parishes of the largest landowners of all, the Laird and clan chiefs, who often either remained Catholic or espoused the Episcopalian Church. These censorious bodies wielded power in several areas—in matters of religious observance, moral behaviour and poor relief, being parochial police and civil administrators as well as religious arbiters. In pursuit of moral rectitude they used the persuasive devices of the times—the stool of repentance, sack cloth garments, jougs and branks, and ridicule—as physical and psychological tools.

During the century the established Church and its ministry were sustained by tithes or levies of a proportion of the crop. In Scotland this was later drawn not in kind but in cash defined by agreed 'fiars rates'. James Anderson comments on the accrued value of tithes from the 'immence tracts' of reclaimed heath during the period 1734 to 1764. This method was claimed to be better than the English mode by which tithes on corn land were payable in kind. The church collections were handicapped by a general scarcity of coins, and near the east coast seaports, by the presence of foreign coins slipped into the collection bags. These were separated out and sold in bulk for their metal value. A common coin in the bags was the Dutch 'doit', worth around 1d. Scots.

While originally the Laird or family chief might have full power of pit and gallows to deal with such serious crime as could escape the 'might is right' inter-clan disputes, the church had to control the day-to-day life and passions of the common people. This it attempted to do—through the Minister with the support and criticism of his elders of the Kirk Session—with great respect for every word of the Bible as interpreted by the few who could read it and with a wholesome fear of Hell after death. The new Catechism ruled and copies of both the long and the short versions had to be kept in the houses of any who could read at all, along with the Confession of Faith. Regardless of rank everyone was examined periodically as to his or her knowledge of the faith. The policies of the congregation were enforced by the beadle, custodian of the jougs, branks and sackcloth, who applied whatever discipline was ordered by the Session. He also patrolled the church during the long tedious sermons, waking sleepers and removing dogs and 'greeting' bairns. Carrying a stick with a cleek he would remove any plaid over a woman's head or any unseemly headgear and in some cases he went so far as to carry a brush and tar to smite the face of anyone found asleep during a long discourse.(25) The moral code was extremely strict. No one was allowed to marry without a guarantee from the Kirk Session of respectability and true adherence to presbyterianism, and money pledges had to be given on their behalf by third parties.

The care of the poor, so long the work of the older Catholic Church, was also one of the most important duties of the Kirk Session in every Parish, for beggars abounded. Even in Catholic times the Act of 1503 had stipulated that none should be allowed to beg except 'crooked folk, seik folk, impotent folk and weak folk'; that 'poor could only beg in their own Parish'; and that 'stray beggars were to be nailed by the ears to a tree and the persistent to have their ears cut off'.(25) But the approach of the reformed church was quite different from that of the Catholic abbeys. The monks, who had stored grain from their grange farms in anticipation of bad harvests, would have dispensed food after supping the cream themselves. With the new regime money was now the vehicle for relief. An elaborate system of controlled begging was instituted and when things got desperate grain was brought in from abroad, the Minister acting as grocer, selling to those who could buy and doling out a little to those who were literally starving and penniless. Relief was well organised. Handicapped and privileged beggars had to wear parish badges and could move from parish to parish with some hope of charity; the unbadged who did not bow to the severe church creed were hounded without mercy from one area to the next. Not only were beggars and local poor thus relieved but special Church collections were made for absent parishioners held captive in distant prisons or by the English army. All this work had to depend on the meagre church collections augmented by fines levied on moral delinquents, for any attempt to levy a general poor rate was strongly resisted. Fines for adultery were a good source of additional revenue for the heavy, strongly padlocked, well guarded poor box.

The trials and tribulations of the churches—and the common people under them—come into particularly sharp focus in areas where both churches were strongly represented. Perthshire and Angus were such areas because of the interpenetration there of the Highland and Lowland cultures, and the records of two parishes there—Kenmore and Auchterhouse—give a good insight into the daily workings of the churches and their impact on the lives of the people. In the Strathmore area the Minister of the Parish of Auchterhouse was the Rev Patrick Johnston, a staunch adherent of the Presbyterian Church; the Parish Church at Kenmore, though nominally a national presbyterian building, was still held by the Rev Alexander Comrie, a strong Episcopalian.

Mr Johnston, educated at St Andrews University, was appointed by the presbytery, not by the congregation or by the Laird, who were by no means Covenanters. At his introduction to the flock a substantial dinner was organised, costing £26.18s. in Scots currency or £2.4s. sterling. Both currencies were valid, while the old copper coins and foreign cash were only fit to be dropped with a satisfying clunk into the collection bag, which was rather thoughtfully constructed to hide one's contribution from inquisitive neighbours. There were no tables for this meal, sawn boards being rarely seen. No women were present and the men, few of whom were kilted, sat around where they could and tore into the meat with their socktilegs or clasped pocket knives. The dirk, today a feature of the Scottish costume, was then far too substantial a weapon to use at a meal, far less to slip into a stocking top for ornament! About 18 inches long with a groove for easy extraction after use it was kept exclusively for serious inter-clan warfare and the occasional foray south of the border. Oatmeal was bought for the occasion along with a boll (16 gallons) of malt. Three sheep were killed and there was baking, but there was no sugar for sweetness, no tea and little which would appeal to modern tastes for such an auspicious occasion.

The Auchterhouse session clerk left behind a very detailed record of this closely disciplined community: 'Thomas Anderson and Eliza Petrie were found guilty of serious misconduct', for which Tom had to do penance and face condemnation and ridicule by standing on the 'pillar'—a raised stool set before the whole congregation—for three Sundays running and there thole an extremely long sermon of condemnation. Poor Eliza was to stand there for the next three in similar plight. William Christie, their employer and a substantial local farmer, was held surety for their attendance by a money penalty of £4 Scots, so that they stood to lose their job and their house in default of attendance.

Elizabeth Whitton, leaving the Parish for another, had to obtain a testimony from the Minister to use as a passport into her new community. At this date such written passports even had to be obtained by people moving into the next Parish on a Sunday so that they could be excused from attendance at their Church and be accepted at another Service 'where they rested on the Sabbath day'.(25)

'John Anderson of Auchrannie paid £3.6s. Scots for his son to be buried in the church.' The church floor of beaten earth covered the bodies of those whose kin could afford the fee. 'March 17th, 1706 Grizell Watson was before the congregation, for going to her mother's house with Ogilvie, younger, of the Peal and staying some time in his company.' Grizell was a young lassie and it was her mother Agnes who was ordered to appear three times on the pillar and be publicly rebuked for her daughter's misdemeanour. Ogilvie, the Laird's nephew, visiting from Lintrathen, appears to have escaped rebuke. The Kirk, relentless, was merely biding its time with Grizell however, and four years later on 4 June 1710 the Presbytery itself got round to fining her '£10 Scots for her scandalous on going with Ogilvie of Peill'.

On 16 August 1706 'John Anderson and others were rebuked for yoking their carts on a sabbath evening,' this for an overnight journey on the Laird's business. All the transport required by the ever-increasing number of the Laird's relatives was carried out by the tenants and this became especially burdensome at seed and harvest times. The Laird's land always had to be ploughed first, and by harvest time a call to cart coal from Dundee to Auchterhouse Castle was far from welcome, causing friction between the legal right of the Laird and the moral views of the Minister and his elders. Four years later when Anderson 'cast seven hundred divots for repairing the school' he received no payment, whether to atone for his earlier transgression or to make up for an old debt by the Laird we do not know.

'David Cuthbert and Patrick Low were "delated" for debating about a bargain in the church yard on the sabbath day' (25) and Thomas Hill who was seen counting and drawing his sheep from David Thain's flock 'on another sabbath, confessed and was rebukt and dismissed'. In such misdemeanours the elders and the beadle formed the police force. They patrolled the area during sermons held not only on the sabbath but on rather frequent 'fast' days, searching the town and the change houses for defaulters who preferred to sup ale rather than suffer sermons.

Having accepted the burden of local education—the busy Minister and his elders acting as School Board—the Kirk was responsible for providing a combined school-and-schoolhouse and for paying the teacher. He—there is no reference in the records to a wife or family—lived in the schoolroom, which was heated by fuel carried by pupils from their homes. The walls were of divot and required rebuilding between the cruik roof trusses from time to time. There were no glazed windows, wall openings with wooden shutters on the lee side being uncovered and those on the windward shut on stormy days. At that date only the church windows had glass, protected by thin iron rods.

The rebellions did not leave the churches unscathed, and although Mr Johnston and the majority of his elders at Auchterhouse were against the uprising, in the neighbouring parish of Newtyle the presbyterian minister Mr Clephane was chased from his church and manse by a band 'hired by a local proprietor' and had to leave the country. This Jacobite laird and his men smashed up the manse and its furnishing, 'sticking their claymores thro' the very bedding, all in the presence of his helpless wife and family'. However the Minister returned after the rebellion was suppressed, 'living to see the principles of his church triumphant', and for those who supported the wrong cause the Kirk's vengeance was not long in coming. At Auchterhouse on 15 March 1716, only one month after James, the Old Chevalier, left the country, Gilbert Mearns was summoned to appear before the Session. The charge was, after the Minister, fearful of his very life, had fled the parish on the gathering of the Jacobite forces, he had 'declared the church vacant and pinned Mar's proclamation to the kirk door calling Scotland to arms to resist the foreign yoke'. Similarly on 15 April William Horn, Gilbert McMillan, William Kininmouth, Dave Lowson and John and James Gillies were also up before the Session. They had rung the kirk bell and built a bonfire when news of James' landing at Peterhead reached Auchterhouse. They had not only rung the bell 'about 10 of the clock at night' but 'committed other insolencies . . . to the great surprise of the parish', they had 'drunk the Pretenders' health and spoken many reproachful words against the King and Government'. Authority was satisfied when they were 'sharply rebuked' from the pulpit.

In the absence of banks the church loaned money to the Laird on the security of the parish, as well as acting as pawnbroker to those in need. Thus when the possession of Auchterhouse passed to Lord Airlie of Cortachy, with it went his predecessor Lord Lyon's liabilities. On 25 December 1716 the Kirk Session received from Lord Airlie £297 and £75 being rent (interest) due by Lord Lyon on the transfer of Auchterhouse to Airlie. With this money they 'paid £144 to the schoolmaster for salary due'. The poor schoolmaster appears to have been without any salary since the start of the rebellion!

After the 1715 rebellion the Auchterhouse Kirk Sesion continued its legislative and administrative activities. On 15 December 1717 it enacted 'that no servant be fee'd (engaged) nor cottars sell without testimonies from the parish from whence they came last'. An innovation occurred in 1728 when seats—to be rented—were erected, in the Church; previously seats were privately constructed with permission and no doubt a fee.

In 1740 there was an extremely bad harvest and that winter and spring many people in the Strathmore area were literally starving. Riots broke out and the Church authorities were hard put to relieve their suffering congregation. On 17 May 1741 'David Johnston of Auchterhouse bought 10 bolls of pease for the use of the poor at £12 Scots per boll. This was put in the Minister's girnal, ground next day and sold by James Crichton.' 'No credit was given without the support of two elders.' 'Poor women to get credit for 1 lb of lint and 6*d*. for their maintenance.' The meal sold for 9½*d*. per peck but '1 boll, 1 firlot and two lippies were given to the poor'.

On 27 October 1747 John Swan paid 5*s*. for absolution from the pillory; John Smith bought a seat in the kirk 'for him and his heirs'. John Anderson died and his burial was arranged by the Minister, who was reimbursed from the kirk funds 'For a coffin 5/-, and a winding sheet 2/6'. Ale cost 5*s*. and a mutchkin of brandy (4 gills) was required costing 6½*d*. The cost of digging the grave was 1*s*.

In Kenmore Parish the story was somewhat different but also typical of the turbulent times. There the Minister, Alexander Comrie, was an Episcopalian and an intimate friend of the Earl of Breadalbane. He too maintained strict discipline, arranging immediately on his appointment for two of the elders to patrol the church area to arrange for appropriate punishment those 'lying about without the church and will not come in to hear the sermon'. He even managed to stop the autumn practice of gathering hazel nuts in the woods on the Sabbath!

Before the 1715 rebellion proclamations from 'King James' (the Old Chevalier) and the Earl of Mar were read from the pulpit. Following the rebellion Comrie was deposed but held the manse and kirk at bay against presbyterian authority for several years, for the local people supported him and when a committee of Presbytery went to Kenmore on 26 September 1721 no one attended church 'although three bells had been rung'. When Comrie finally handed over, his successor John Hamilton, ordained on 4 June 1723, had great difficulty in establishing himself since the elders and most of the congregation refused to attend church with a Presbyterian Minister. His stipend was paid in small amounts by the tenants, some of whom lived 17 miles away and he had to ride out to these people to collect it personally. Since some of them were two years in arrears and he had no power to enforce payment, 'It is a great drudgery for me to uplift it.' Furthermore he was boycotted by the congregation and by his elders, and many of the Church possessions—the communion cups, the kirk box, the bible, the mort cloth, etc— were still held by Mr Comrie and the elders. By October 1723 he had recruited two of the old elders but was still trying to get the keys to the kirk box. Ultimately at a meeting at Taymouth Castle in December Mr Comrie was forced to hand over the keys and church possessions to a committee, and the church settled into its normal routine.

Five years later on 22 December 1728 Patrick Campbell Vintner 'sat with the elders by virtue of an order from the Earl of Breadalbane's Commissioners'. His place was to 'oblige any who might prove contumacious to the Session in the exercise of their discipline, to be obsequious'. On 23 November 1729 the Session paid the smith for making 'shakels' for John McNicol, a madman. On 23 April 1729 'the session went about privy censures'. The elders and the beadle 'were removed one by one' and the 'usual questions were proposed to them'; 'Their life and conversation were enquired into.' 'Nothing was found but what was savourey.' On 29 October 1732 the mort cloth had been given out for the funeral of George Robertson's mother. He was only charged half a crown because 'the session of Weem have got a far better one of fine velvet'. The Kenmore one was only plush! On 25 August 1734 the Minister 'saw a printed recommendation in favour of Christian Hardy, a Turk born in Smyrna and taken by the Spaniards and robbed', who had turned Christian. He got five shillings sterling from the session.

On 27 April 1735, obsolete coins continuing to be a nuisance, David Walker, treasurer, 'sold to John McIlontie, tinkard in the west end, nine pounds and a half of bad sanded copper babies' (presumably a local spelling of 'baw bees', the Scots halfpence) 'which were of no manner of use, for one pound seven shillings'— a loss of seven pounds thirteen shillings and six pennies Scots.

On 11 May 1735 the afternoon service was not held in the Church but at Taymount Castle, 'The Earl having a sore leg and could not come to Church and my Lord Monzie likewise being there.'

On 24 June 1744 four pound Scots was collected as ransom

money for John Anderson 'in slavery in Tangiers', and a house-to-house collection by the Minister, Mr John Douglas, raised sterling for the Royal Infirmary in Edinburgh. On 9 April 1749 the Session met to consider the payments made to the beadle for his duty in rounding up delinquents, and did ordain 'for every summons east of Ardtalnaig or east of Lawers, 40 pennies Scots'; for 'any in Ardtalnaig, Lawers or Glen Queach a half merk; for every one who mounts the pillar for single fornication, 20 pennies; for a relapse in fornication, half a merk; for a trilapse of adultery ten shillings Scots'. For attendance on and service to the Session he got four pounds Scots yearly, plus extra at Sacraments.

In July the Minister heard that certain people in the Parish had been guilty of 'prophaning the Lords Day' by setting out with their horses and creels to cart coal to Taymount Castle from Alloa, this being a free transport at the Laird's calling. The journey had been started 'in fair daylight'. The elders had met at Lawers and 'expressed their detestation of such open and daring prophanation of the Lords Day'. The tenants concerned appeared and admitted that 'they set off their servants and horses that Sunday before the sun set'. They 'confessed themselves guilty of sin', 'professed their sorrow and repentance', and 'promised to walk more christianly and circumspectly.' The Session rebuked them, the rebuke being intimated in Church the following Sunday.

On 3 July 1752 the Session agreed to license all beggars and provide them with badges to certify their indigent circumstances. Any getting charity 'out of the box' to dispone to the Kirk all their goods and effects 'at the hour of their death'. In 1757 the Kirk Session of Kenmore complained that the Kirk Session of Killin was not taking care of its own poor, there were two kirk sessions in this Parish, and a memorial was sent.

Throughout his tenure Mr Hamilton of Kenmore was very active in starting schools in the outlying parts of his wide-spread parish, for 'people were clamouring for education for their children'. Tenant farmers' children were taught to read; day labourers' children got no education at all. Three shillings Scots were 'Paid to Patrick Forbes who taught a school in the Milltown of Artalnaig and who was poor' and Daniel McNaughton, a soldier, and his spouse Margaret Campbell 'Kept school at

Ballynatibert'—in this period women retained their pre-marriage title rather than their husband's surname.

A fine (mulct) on John McGrigor, 'four pounds Scots, was given to John Campbell of Mutton hole to pay his Board and as recompense for presenting in Irish (Gaelic)'. John Campbell, his son, got two shillings sterling to buy a bible, to learn to read, but he was 'not to sell it, dispose of it, or any for him'. Practically all school textbooks were bibles, catechisms or religious books. Many family heirlooms of this kind were in fact school reading books rather than the family's religious library.

On the application of Ewan MacDougall, elder, and his brother John, the people at Artalnaig, who wished to set up an itinerant schoolmaster in their district, were promised 'the first and the readiest mulct, for their encouragement in so good and pious a design.' Lawers also wanted some of these 'pecunial mulcts' for educational purposes.

One of the problems of schooling in the Highlands was the almost complete lack of bridges by which the pupils could gain access to schools. Fording the burns and rivers was done on horseback but children required a bridge. This was a special problem since all trees had long been cut down and no planting had yet been done. Thus, 'Trees for a bridge were provided by the Lairds of Wester Shian and Turreich while the Kirk Session of Kenmore paid for its erection.' The school at Struan required a bridge over the Erochtie. The Duke of Atholl offered trees from Rannoch but transport was too difficult. The Blair Atholl Kirk Session solved the problem by offering a shilling sterling 'for each tree that could be dug out of the peat bogs'. There was as yet no thought of masonry bridges.

School hours were 7–11 and 1–5 in summer and 9–12 and 1–3 in winter. Boys outnumbered girls by ten to one; it was the end of the century before a two to one ratio was established. Teachers were very poorly paid, 'except for their chance at Hansel Monday and cock fighting'. A teacher might move from house to house for board and in return he 'taught at night in every house he came to'.

9 FARMS AND FARMING

The new system evolves

James Donaldson, writing with hindsight in 1794 in his *General View of Agriculture in Banffshire*, gives us a vivid picture of the early days of farming in the North of Scotland. 'No improvements were made to agriculture prior to 1748.' 'Prior to that all the country was farmed in run-rig strips by many individuals working communally and practising the infield and outfield system. The infield near the houses grew oats, bear and pease.'

The transition between run-rig cultivation and level ground husbandry was gradual and sporadic, varying from area to area according to natural endowment and local custom. The key was the Laird who might be in touch with the totally different English practice and often employed an English overseer to encourage level cultivation and the use of the new crops. This may appear strange to Scottish traditions. In the following century however, the practice was reversed and it was the Scottish farmers and overseers who went south to make a success in England, largely because they took with them a tradition of much harder working conditions which they then applied to the more advanced farming technique. Then, following the Laird's example, came the new-style tenant farmers, gradually acquiring expertise and more land and eliminating their contemporaries in the process. Furthermore the two approaches to farming might even exist side by side on the same estate, the new being tried out on the Laird's home farm, the old practised elsewhere by his tenants or their people.

The first to farm in the English style in the Banff area appears to have been the Earl of Findleter. Impressed by what he had seen in his travels in Southern England he brought north an

English overseer who began transforming his estate as early as 1748. The first step was to reduce the number of people on the land, and three out of four families were cleared off. The loss of so many men at Culloden only three years before simplified this—who cared then where the widows and families moved, except for the city manufacturers who welcomed the cheap female labour? The survivors on the land were now in competition with each other to become the new race of tenant farmers, employing their less acquisitive fellows. Farming was to be an industry rather than a subsistence way of life. The new methods produced a surplus of crop to be sold and by this time there was a market for the extra produce which would bring in cash, most of which would find its way into the larger landowners' pockets.

Thus the Findleter estates progressed, leading the northern landowners to a new way of life. The Earl set about granting leases of two periods of nineteen years, or a lifetime, to selected tenants, giving them exclusive right—previously held by four or more families—to areas of arable land. These new tenants had to enclose at their own cost and by their own labour a stipulated part of their new farm tenancy. This was enclosed and divided into the new pattern of fenced fields and prodigious amounts of labour were expended in levelling these. All this area had to be broken in during the first nineteen years. By then the selected farmer, now past middle age, would set about breaking in and enclosing the remainder of his holding. If, unfortunately for his family but to the benefit of the landowner, he died during this period, the lifetime rental automatically expired and the Laird was free to capitalise on the family's efforts and begin again with a new tenant at an enhanced rent. In any event when the thirty-eight years expired the old man, if still surviving, would see the fruits of his work pass to the original owner. Just as the early clearances had been conducted largely with goodwill, all this was done in the name of progress in a gentlemanly and punctilious manner, and many concessions were made to favoured families.

The new factors laid down strict rules as to how the land was to be cultivated and with what crops, so that the new farmers were not only told what to do but also well warned not to conduct their operations in any way which would offend the Laird or be against his interests. They could not crop their land every year lest it should be impoverished; they were bound to summer fallow, thus losing a cash crop of oats or barley; and during the first five years they had to sow a stipulated acreage in grass seeds. This was indeed an innovation for up to that time grass had appeared naturally when the land lay derelict. A new-fangled vegetable, the turnip, was introduced. It was many years before the new methods became general, even on the estate farm. Once started however they gained impetus and like the levelled rigs and the displaced families the old style of farming was soon forgotten.

In similar vein when the Duke of Atholl cleared the ferm toun of Over Benchil, near Stanley, forfeited by the Nairns after the 1745 rebellion and let it to John Stewart of Shierglass in 1790, it was partitioned into thirteen bracks (fields) of some 10–12 acres each. The tack (lease) stipulated that 'the land was not again to be subdivided'. Atholl retained the right to plant up to 8 acres in trees and did not allow Stewart to cast or burn any divots off the moorland 'on penalty of one penny per divot'. He was bound 'to hinder all poachers of game', the woods were to be fenced and the fences kept sheep-proof. Stewart was to be paid £7.10s.0d. yearly for 'making the enclosures and training the hedgerows and hedgerow trees' but the Duke provided gates and gateposts. In addition to all this Stewart had to build a complete new steading but got £100 thereto from the Duke, who also supplied roof timbers from his own plantation, one of the first to be planted in the area.

Late in the century then, despite very sharp differences between one region and another, the fields were level and enclosed, and the infield-outfield system had disappeared. There were far fewer cattle on the hills and lowlands alike and more grain was being grown; there were new crops and cropping methods. The glens, still with access to the hill pastures, were using little or no fallow and growing all the grain they could while the Lowlands, deprived of the hill ground, had to grow fodder for their animals for summer as well as winter feed. Soon as much as half of the land on the new style farms was in grass to maintain the growing demand for meat from cattle or sheep. (12) An average farm in Angus, by then around 200 acres in size, had 100 acres grass, 40 acres oats, 40 barley, 20 faliow, potatoes, turnips or peas. In the eastern areas of the country the practice of rotation had been fully developed and might consist of fallow, wheat, then peas or beans, followed by barley sown with grass, then green feed or hay; finally an oat crop would complete the six year crop rotation.(12)

As their zeal for improved farming grew apace, estate managers tried to control the agricultural techniques of their tenants. For example Stobhall Estate near Perth, backward in many ways, abhorred weeds, and this led to the singular practice there of 'Riding the Guild'. The object of the exercise was to eliminate the corn marigold (chrysanthemum segetum), a conspicuous and gregarious arable weed. Certain farms in the area were administered by a Guild and on a specified day in August the Guild members patrolled the fields of the farmers under their control. For every stalk of the corn marigold they found, the negligent farmer was fined one penny.(35) Ironically, this practice meant that while the Guild lands were free of this plant the nearby fields were infested.

Cropping regulations enforceable by the Sheriff were also established, not only between tenant and tacksman and later between tenant and factor but particularly between outgoing and ingoing tenants. Tenants bound by such regulations (called 'Tirds' or 'Twirds') were bound not to take successive crops off the outfield.(31) Another stipulation was not to fourth crop it till the 'haugh ley'—the ley or grass crop off land not dunged at 6 years old—failing which an outgoing tenant would claim damages before the Sheriff against the ingoing tenant for illegal husbandry.(31)

But these were only the pinpricks. As farms were being formed and enclosed 'poor cultivators were being expelled', sub-letting was forbidden, and rural areas once thronging with people were being emptied. 'Sub-letting in the past had caused much oppression of the poor and weak by the strong.'(36) As a further instance of this policy, no tenant in the Loch Tayside area could hold more than one farm,(36) which meant that the landlord could get rid of all the odd bits of land held by his followers in adjacent 'farms'. In this case forty notices to quit were served in 1795 and 'many of those who were removed ultimately found their way to Canada'. That there was progress and improve-ment—as seen on a broader canvas and in a long perspective—

is undeniable but the immediate human cost was immense and largely unrecorded.

The farm and its economy

What was the 'farm' like as it emerged from this process of evolution? The term encompassed a wide range of conditions which we should at least sample in order to get our feet on the ground. McArthur(11) tells of the farm of Blarigaw on Loch Tayside in 1770. This farm of 290 acres was worked by tenants, but also supported three crofts. Each of the tenants held an ox-gang of land, and 'the infields varied from $1\frac{1}{2}$ acres to 9 acres so that they had to be cropped in strips'. The outfield holdings similarly varied from 1 to 11 acres. All the tenants combined to plough the inbye land but each thereafter looked after his own ground. There were 40 to 50 acres of meadow, 20 to 30 acres grass and a few acres of woodland. In addition to all these, very complex rights to the use of small individual patches of the rocky Ben Lawers hillside had been built up over the years, although these rights were soon to be swept away in the lowland clearances.

Another example is the farm of Stron Fearman, also in Loch Tayside, an area of $324\frac{1}{2}$ acres which had at that time four communal ploughs worked by the ten families of subtenants. In addition there were seven cotteries and one croft, giving a total of eighteen families—perhaps one hundred people.(11) But the situation was much more complex than it may appear. First Stron Fearman included 35 acres which were in dispute with the nearby farm of Port of Loch Tay. Secondly and typically, one subtenant, Archibald Cameron, not only held as tenant one-tenth of Stron Fearman but also held $7\frac{1}{2}$ acres at Tayinloan farm and worked one-half of the 53 acres of Croft-in-Loan farm, which is not surprising in view of the fact that Stron Fearman held only 52 acres of arable infield (to be shared by ten tenants). And lastly, all had access to free grazing on the nearby slopes of the Ben Lawers mountain range, although these were shared out among several farms and estates and quite possibly with people in lowland areas as a detached portion of their own lowland parish. A complex of interdependencies indeed!

The composition of the 'farm' from a functional point of view was as follows—52 acres of annually cultivated land in permanent rigs; 20 acres of outfield land cropped only occasionally when it had built up some fertility; 21 acres of grassland intermingled with the run-rigs; 10 acres of oak wood whose use was controlled by the estate; 2 acres of 'mead'— possibly boggy land; and 220 acres of uncultivatable lands claimed by the tenants as their own, the higher parts of which McArthur describes as 'strong heath' practically indistinguishable from the hill grazing on the other side of the hill dyke. Most of this consisted of grass and muirfield, overgrown to some extent by hazel bushes which were allowed to grow for their use as wattle and basket material. Beside the streams in the bogland were alder trees—again an essential part of the residents' requirements for house construction, for in the absence of planted trees any naturally sown tree surviving to maturity was treasured. The 'fields' of this 'farm', themselves split into separately claimed strips, ran from 1 to 17 acres and lay in the 'plain and hollows' between the hills.(11) The whole area was stoney and full of rocks while on the east side of the farm the ground was very steep. Such were the living areas of the Breadalbane clansmen of the mid-eighteenth century.

As an example of conditions in the lowlands consider an arable farm in Menteith of 140 acres, a small farm by modern standards. This farm comprised 94 acres of carse ground and 46 acres of 'dry field', and though tenanted and cultivated by one family as a unit it still included sub-tenants. Married men were employed on the farm as well as day labourers and tradesmen. These essential workers were allowed to retain for their own use a small area of land—toft, croft, pendicle or yard—on which they would raise the essentials for their families' sustenance— milk, food grain as oats, peas or barley and later potatoes. The meagre cash payment made to them at long intervals by the farmer would be essential for such goods as could not be produced at home.

A farm of this size, which today can be worked by one family with occasional help, required the labour of about ten land workers, eight of them resident on the farm with their families. However this number of thirty to forty people was still a reduction from the run-rig days. There would be two married ploughmen, and another unmarried man would live in or near the farmhouse but would be fed by the farmer's staff of two maids. These men would be paid around £7 per annum, the senior obtaining some £2 extra as grieve or supervisor. The women, who would normally live in the farmhouse, would receive about £3.10s.0d. per annum plus one pair of shoes, while an outworker woman, or day labourer was paid 8d. per day. Additional staff comprised a barnman to wield the flail—soon to be obsolete—at £7 per annum and two boys at £5 and £3 respectively plus one pair of shoes each year. The men had their pendicle or grazing for one cow and did not pay rent in cash or kind; those who did not have a pendicle on the farm received an allowance of oat or barley meal sufficient for their family's needs, plus milk. Apart from food produced on the farm the cost to the farmer of labour at £35 per annum amounted to one-sixth of his rent of £210 per annum.

In addition to all these people the farm supported a heavy stock of work animals. There were seven horses for ploughing and carting plus a riding horse, and to maintain the equine establishment, perhaps two colts. Some eight milch cows were further necessary and nine young cattle were carried to support and eventually replace the farm stock, although some would be sold off the farm. To meet the cost of external expenditures, including rent, black cattle from the Highlands were bought in occasionally when feed was available on the farm, to be sold in spring. All these animals consumed a lot of otherwise saleable produce and required a considerable acreage of land for themselves. On the other hand the dung they produced improved both land and crops.

As regards cash crops for sale off the farm two fields totalling 23 acres produced wheat, and two more of 21 acres, barley. Several crops were produced essentially for consumption by man or beast on the farm: oats from three fields of 27 acres in total; beans, a useful crop on heavy coarse land, from 9 acres; fruit from 16 acres of orchards and plantations. This left two fields of hay (17 acres) and two (25 acres) in pasture. Such was the lack of humus in the soil that one or two fields—about 15 acres—were left fallow each year. About 50 chalders (400 imperial quarts) of lime was applied to the farm each year and 600–700 carts of dung were taken out. (31) By this date in the lowlands cattle were over-wintered inside, the sheep being outdoors.

In passing, Lord Kames reports (1765) that a tenant farmer in

Central Scotland, who would need about £36 to £40 per annum
to maintain his way of life over and above the food and clothes
he got from the farm, was generally considered to be equal in
status to a shopkeeper or manufacturer. By comparison school-
masters got about £35 per annum but without the benefits of
food and clothing which were available to the farmer, while the
parish Ministers of the period received £115 per annum all in.

Farm buildings

The evolution of the farm 'steading'—a word now denoting the
farm buildings proper, which was used towards the end of the
century to describe the 'farm house and offices'(17)—was
extremely erratic both in place and in time. Many of the early
steadings 'were built of stones laid in clay, beaten up and
tempered and covered with thatch and divot' and 'were exceedingly bad'.(14) Many could have been of wattle construction. In earlier times it was customary to house the cattle in the
same building or room as the family, mainly for the sake of the
excellent central heating system provided by the cattle in the
cold winters. The family cow and the dogs were welcome not
only for their bodily presence but also because the manure from
the cow, left inside to heat and decompose, provided additional
warmth. Even in a lean-to, wattle shelter against the house walls
animals helped to insulate the primitive dwelling. By this time,
of course, the bulk of the trees had been destroyed, coal was too
costly—except for the lairds—because of transport costs, and
peat was relatively slow to be utilised. Thus the most common
fuel by the early eighteenth century was divot off uncultivated
land and even this was difficult to keep dry.

Storage of grain was more difficult to accommodate in
dwellings. Unlike house walls, which had to be impervious, barn
walls which withstood rain but allowed a drying wind to pass
were advantageous for hay, particularly on the west coast. Thus
Donald Sage(6) tells of wickerwork barns at Loch Carron
around 1715. These early wicker structures provided shelter for
the sheaves of grain as well as the hay crop, for oats and barley
were not stacked in the farmyard as in the east. Stone walling
with draught-inducing openings like the North of England's

'shippons' was never developed to any extent in Scotland, apart from the remarkable cleits of St Kilda.

Towards the end of the century not only the farm but the modern steading was beginning to take shape. The workers' houses were now placed some distance from the main tenant's dwelling (the farmhouse), which remained close to the buildings housing his stock. The barn would be built on the west side of the steading to catch the wind so essential for winnowing of the chaff. The flail was still being used to separate the grain from the straw, but 'fanners'—hand-operated machines designed to create a draught over the grain—were just coming in. When carts came into use the cart shed would face with its open end to the south. In the early steadings there were no courts or foddering yards, the stock being tied up and stall-fed, and the dung from the stables and cow houses, built to the north of the steading block, was piled in the middle of the yard and left over winter. In Angus, where the early transition buildings had been haphazard in location, the evolving plan had the main buildings forming a square with barns, byres and sheds for cattle.

By this time barns 16 feet wide and 30 to 35 feet long were being constructed and these would have stone walls and roofs of imported timber. Lofts over the buildings were generally not possible, largely because of a lack of load-bearing timbers at an economic cost, and so all the buildings were low, even the barn walls being no more than seven to eight feet high. However in some of the more advanced buildings in the lowland area there began to be a second storey in order that the grain could be stored clear of the ground and thus be less liable to deterioration. Gradually the barn loft became capable of holding a stack of oats at one end, leaving the middle third for threshing and the far end for winnowing the grain.(24) The evolution of the two-storey barn is confirmed by Wight who tells of a Mr Lawson at Mill of Balloch who has 'erected a barn with walls so high that corn can be threshed on the upper floor'. This would be around 1770 when the hand-operated flail (Figure 7) was still in universal use. A steading such as that described including a dwelling house for the farmer would cost about £300 or one to two years' rental.(12)

Thus while *The General View of Southern Perth* in 1794 could say 'On the more progressive farms the houses were being built of

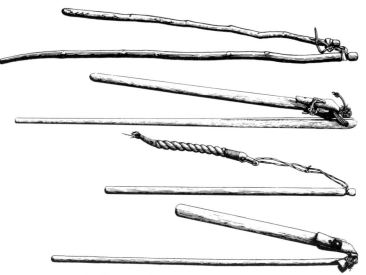

7   Flails, used to thresh oats and barley.

stone and lime, with the farm buildings forming a square behind the farm house with the dung yard in the centre', at the same time it was reporting that the evolution of the farm steading was slow.

Rents, costs and the joys of land ownership

In the early days tenant farmers paid most of their rent in kind— in grain, geese and hens, butter and cheese, and services such as transporting goods and supplying and maintaining all the estate's ploughs and even killing axes. But even before the enclosing of farm land the lairds were starting to sell off land to acquire cash and the luxuries money could now buy. Thus just before the rebellion in 1745 a Clackmannanshire estate amounting to 500 English acres was sold for £7,000 and again in 1759 for £10,000.(14) Furthermore by this date instead of payment in kind the landowners were insisting on cash tenancies, and in 1763 the new owner was able to let the land to a tenant for two terms of nineteen years each, the first at £400, the second at £500 per annum. The Laird's factor and his lawyer helpers made other onerous conditions; at his own cost the new tenant had to enclose the land with suitable fences, walls or hedge and ditch. However he did not try to do this himself nor to cultivate the land under his own direction. Out of the surviving inhabitants on the estate, plus a few incomers driven south from more inhospitable areas yet possessed of some cash or credit, he was able to select nine or ten families who not only took on the burden of enclosure but also paid him 35s. to £2.2s.0d. per acre for the privilege of working the land. Those remaining in the area had to work as labourers or clear off. Thus the new capitalist land user made an adequate profit on his investment, while the new Laird, no longer a clan chief but an incomer, had a more than adequate profit margin on his investment plus the status value of being a large landowner; the estate was his, he could ride and shoot on it as he pleased and could dictate the way of life of its inhabitants.

Sufficient entrepreneur farm speculators were not always forthcoming and the lairds themselves then had to take a share in the capital investment necessary for land cultivation. In some areas 'steelbow' letting was practised whereby the Laird provided and rented not only the land but also the stock so that working farmers could operate without having to have the capital necessary for acquiring cattle.(20) In purely arable areas another system evolved in mid century called 'half foot' tenancies. Here the Laird or the principal tenant provided the land and the seed grain, while the farmer worked the land and reaped the harvest—handing half the crop over to his superior. These arrangements were closely monitored to prevent the farmer from profiting unduly by them. The harvest of grain was closely measured and care was taken not to let the farmer get an undue proportion even of the straw, which would otherwise go to the Laird to feed and bed the home farm cattle. He was not allowed by the lease to thatch his house with straw, but must use reeds or heather in order to preserve the straw as animal feed stuff; he was forbidden to make graddan bread lest he use up straw in the process of scorching the grain prior to milling it in the quern for his own use.(20) Penny pinching as this may seem, it was in keeping with the official doctrine of the period, for no less than Lord Kames in 1775 maintained that a tenant farmer should only live reasonably comfortably on his holding; he was not expected to do any more than this, far less make a profit. It was also in keeping with the times, when it was quite a feat to make a good living at all.

With accommodation and food obtained at home many

farmers towards the end of the century were relatively well off, as evidenced by the high standard of the farm houses then being built and the already high status of the new class of large farmers. This was in vast contrast to the houses and the way of life of their labourers and even more to the squalid homes of the earlier cultivators, for remnants of the old regime still existed alongside the new. Lord Kames (1765) tells that 'in some of the lower areas' a farm of 104 acres, the old ploughgate measure previously occupied by many more families, was now being worked as a single-plough farm by three or four tenants each paying a rent of £5 per annum. Gradually with improved implements and stronger, better fed horses this agricultural unit became a two-pair farm worked by a farmer, his family and a day labourer paid 8d. per working day. We might note in passing on the durability of common measures in the face of technical obsolescence. The common yardstick of relative size had already in some cases changed from the plough to the number of pairs of horses required to operate the area, although the ploughgate as a unit of area remained. In turn the pair as a unit was to continue until well after the introduction of tractors and the departure of horses from the agricultural scene.

The capital cost of equipping such a farm was then reckoned at about £75(24) although Lord Kames curiously did not include cattle in this, even the milch cow necessary for family sustenance. This reckoning was as follows:

4 horses @ £12	£48
Harness	2
2 new style ploughs @ £1	2
2 carts	14
Harrows and a brake	2
Wooden roller	1
Fanner	2
Forks, scythe and a barrow	1.10.0
12 'harden' (coarse linen) grain sacks	2
	£74.10

Annual expenses were reckoned on the lines of the next table, and again it is interesting that Lord Kames makes no allowance in his calculations for interest on the farmer's capital, the latter was not expected to make a profit, only to have a better livelihood than his labourers!!

Capital depreciation 20% of £74.10	£14.18
Farmer's wages/living expenses	20
Labourer's wages	12
Horses' maintenance (feed)	24
Extra labour for harvest, shearing, etc	8
Seed	10
	£88.18

The value of the produce off this new style single-family farm was estimated by Lord Kames at £155. Sixty acres of the newly levelled and enclosed ground would be put into corn crop producing 5 bolls to the acre at 50s. per boll = £150. In addition the farmer would be able to overwinter ten cattle brought in after harvest and sold in spring at an average profit of 10s. per animal = £5. Total income £155. Deducting expenditure of £88.18s.0d. would leave a 'profit' of £66.2s. This sum Lord Kames considered the suitable rent payable to the landowner!

Interesting as those figures may be in terms of social equity their full significance is seen only if we compare the new farm tenancy with the earlier system whereby four farmers shared the ground at a rental of £5 each. The increased profit to the landowner and the incentive to him to promote the new style of farming is obvious. But this involved halving yet again the farm population, who were already the survivors of an original farm population of possessors and tenants four times larger. Much has been made of the Highland Clearances, but the largely unremarked Lowland clearances had removed more than half the rural population of Scotland twice within fifty years, all in the name of progress. The new factories got ample cheap labour, the colonies manpower and who cared for starving beggars roaming the countryside?

10   CROPS AND THEIR USE

In the run-rig days the two parts of the farm, the inbye and the
outbye, received quite different treatment—a practice which
served to perpetuate and increase the difference between them.
The inbye was cropped in grain year in, year out, the normal
cropping schedule being one year in barley and two years in oats.
The outbye was cropped only intermittently. Later more
modern practices crept in, encouraged in every way by the
Commissioners of the Forfeited Estates. Summer fallowing was
advocated and wheat production was practised in favoured
areas. Lord Kames stated 'Oats had to be sown in March; if that
month was wet, then the best plan was to summer fallow and sow
in autumn with wheat.'
   The outfield was treated in an entirely different way from the
infield area. Here some three or four successive crops of oats were
taken. It was then allowed to relapse into a poor pasture of weeds
and grass to recover fertility for another cycle of cropping. This
was achieved by grazing with stock, which were continually
herded all day by the young girls and boys of the community. At
night they were herded into small enclosures.

Grain

The runrig cultivators depended for their very existence on
personal consumption of practically all the grain they grew on
their limited holdings: little or none was to spare for export or for
feed to poultry or swine, and if there was a surplus it was made
into whisky or ale. 'Bere' was sown on the best of the outfield
land, but as time went on this was displaced by the more
developed form of barley *hordeum distichon*, and in 1790 the
commentator for Criesh(33) reports that 'much barley was
grown, formerly it was all bere, but now bere is going out fast and

barley taking over'. Barley, while extensively used for bannocks, was not used as porridge, and the kernel-removing technique of making 'Pearl' barley for soup was still in the distant future.

Oats had long been grown in Scotland: writing in the eighteenth century Donaldson claims that Caithness in 1695 exported 16,000 bolls of grain, and Ferguson in praising the good estate management and natural fertility of that county claimed it to be one of the best grain-growing areas in Scotland.

Wheat was grown on the estate-run farms in the Carse of Stirling in West Perthshire in 1775. In these heavy clay lands it was a labour-intensive crop which took two years to reach harvest. Preparations began in May after the barley crop was sown, when the wheat ground was first ploughed and water-furrowed. Then early in June the 'great brake' was put on in an endeavour to kill off as much weed growth as possible, and in July a second ploughing took place, this time 'against the ridges' with water-furrowing again. This was followed by three more applications of the brake and two harrowings before dung was applied and the ground limed. After a last harrowing the seed was sown in September or early October.(24) By this time the crop had involved almost six months of soil preparation, and the ground was actually gone over no less than twelve times before the crop even germinated. After all that it is rather a relief to know that 'where wheat was sown on loamy soils there was no need for water furrowing'!(24)

Peas

On the run-rig settlements peas were widely cultivated, peasemeal being a welcome though unappetising alternative to oats for porridge or brose. The fertilising value of peas as a crop had been well recognised in the previous century, as witness an Act of 1685 'Requiring all persons (in the said shire of Aberdeen) who shall hereafter labour ground for corn shall sow yearly the twentieth part of their infield or croft land with peas and beans or peas alone and the thirtieth part of the said infield or croft land if the ground be ane muirland sown and that under pain and penalty of ten pounds for every boll of the said peas and beans that shall not be sown.'(17)Towards the end of the century peas as a soil conditioner were displaced by red clover.

Broom

Whins and broom, both legumes and both with soil improving virtues, were grown and cherished as a crop: their value as cattle food in the absence of turnips or as winter shelter for cattle and horses was considerable. 'Broom was not to be cut without the permission of the Laird.' (36) Whins were well bruised by the use of a flail to make them edible by stock, and well into the end of the century whin mills were still being erected on enclosed farms to ease the cost of employing men for that task. The mill comprised a round stone set on edge and rotated by gearing operated by a horse. The end product was considered good food and was relished by oxen and horses.(13)

On the new style farms special fields, which still carry the name 'Broom Park', were often set aside for the sowing of broom, and in Angus and the Mearns nearly every farm had such a field. The broom was not crushed like whins but was allowed to grow 6 to 8 feet high, then during severe winters the black cattle were let into these fields to browse on the thinner branches and leaf twigs. The broom park was well tended and a crop would last seven to eight years before requiring renewal, becoming so rampant in extreme cases as to allow furniture to be made of the main stems! Examples of this clear yellow woodwork, which was valued for its colour and durability, are to be seen at Blair Castle in Perthshire. At the end of its life the broom normally provided firewood and was considered the ideal fuel for bannock-making, providing a quick sharp heat that could be regulated easily. Apart from being crushed for winter feed whins were also sown for sheep grazing, some being grown as hedging material until required during a hard spell of weather. The seeds for these crops were imported from England and Ireland. Whins were very extensively grown as cattle feed in Galloway where the northern black cattle were finally finished off for the English market and the winter survival of the stock in good condition was very important.(20)

Turnips

The growing of turnips as a field crop was responsible for much of the change in agriculture in the later years of the eighteenth century, particularly in the development of cattle-rearing. Nevertheless it was slow and erratic. Turnips were grown in the Banff area as early as 1748 but could not be grown in nearby Aberdeenshire until nearly the end of the century due to the absence of fenced enclosures for protection against grazing stock. They were grown much more extensively in the more progressive areas such as Strathmore and the Lothians. Because of the turnip fly as a pest it was considered that this crop could only be grown on moorland areas which had not previously had a turnip crop, namely the outbye lands of the earlier cultivators. Naturally this land required a great deal of preparation and in West Perthshire by the 1760–90 period it was being 'cross ploughed five times, dunged and sown with turnips', this being followed in due course by oats and in the third year by clovers and rye grass.

Potatoes

Potatoes were one of the new crops appearing in Scotland in the eighteenth century, and it appears that the first potatoes came to Edinburgh from England about 1720 and also to the west coast from Ireland. This new crop had been introduced to Ireland in 1590 by Sir Walter Raleigh and its use very quickly spread throughout the whole of that country and thence to Kirkcudbright in 1725. Potatoes were extensively grown in the lowlands by 1739 but their spread to the north and west was relatively slow. By 1775 West Perthshire farmers getting crops of 3 to 4 tons per acre were making ready sales to the burgh towns where already the craftsmen were finding it more profitable to sell or feu off their plots than to grow their own food thereon.

To begin with the potatoes were only available for eating from July to December when frost spoiled those left above ground or in the unheated houses.(14) Soon however those stored in the barn under straw or below a stack of oats were found to be still edible and this cheap food could then be used until April. The seed potatoes however were still stored in a hole in the ground mixed with sand and dry leaves with a stack of hay or corn on top. Soon it was discovered that a late crop could be obtained by planting in June so that in the following spring the less advanced tubers did not sprout so readily.(24) Thus as time went on strains or varieties were selected out and early or late types evolved, and when Pennant made his tour in 1770 he reported that 'potatoes were grown in every garden', a fact whose social significance should not be underplayed. With this prolific plant much less land and labour were needed to feed a family, making land more profitable and people less necessary and thus further facilitating the clearances.

In passing, a story from the Western Isles illustrates the problems that can beset any innovation however benign. In 1743 old Clanranald and his men from the Hebrides were over in Ireland visiting his relative MacDonell of Antrim. There they saw and sampled potatoes for the first time. The old man approved of this new food and thought it well worthy of adoption by his clansmen, although the lads were not so sure about this strange alternative to brose. However Clanranald filled his boat and brought them back to Uist, and summoning his tenants he instructed them as to the planting technique. When they flatly refused to have anything whatever to do with the strange things Clanranald, enraged, clapped them in prison to consider his proposal further. They finally agreed under protest, were released and according to instructions made the first lazy-beds on good cas chrom cultivated soil, where the curious plants grew and ripened. Of course the shaws were unedible, so the tubers were then dug up. But to eat anything from below the surface was an affront to the pious Highlanders, so the whole crop was taken back to the laird's castle. Dumping the lot on his lordship's doorstep they firmly declared that though he might force them to grow the detested things he could not force them to eat them. However once the cooking process had been demonstrated some tried them out and eventually they were accepted as an article of diet. Progress was slow however; it took nine years before the men in the adjoining Isle of Barra tried them out and began to plant them.

Grass and hay

As a departure from the earlier reliance on chance natural seeding in the outbye areas the management of pasture land for grass and hay only began towards the end of the century as the remnants of the run-rig system disappeared. With the introduction of large sheep flocks on the hill grazings it was found that frequent burning of the natural heath climax vegetation, which started in the Peebles area, produced 'a tender growth excellent pasture for sheep'.(33) So effective was this early 'management' that the alpine type meadow soon vanished from the mountains and eventually poor fire-resistant strains of grass became dominant, greatly reducing the food value of the pasturage. The virtual elimination of the crofters' small black cattle and the massive introduction of the new breeds of sheep completed the transformation. The Victorian grouse-shooting landowners who followed arrested the process by encouraging the heather on the northern and mid-Scotland hillsides but on many of the lower mountain ranges the process was irreversible.

The next step was to do something to improve the outfield areas. First some effort was made, once wood floors were available in the new granaries or hay lofts, to save the natural grass seed for hand sowing; the next step was to select a definite type of grass for the process. Johnston's edition of *Gerald's Herbal* drew attention to a grass called 'Red Darnell' (*lolium temulentum*), a stout erect annual native of southern Europe which was introduced to England as 'Rye grass' and sown there in 1673.(35) Red clover and others were also introduced. Soon autumn sowing of rye grass and clover as a field crop was being advised and clover was also being sown with flax. The Commissioners of the Forfeited Estates were early to note the advantage of this new style of farming and by Lord Kames' time red clover, white clover, yellow clover, rye grass and the narrow leaved plantain, ribwort, were being sown. By then Kames was advocating that on a properly run farm there should be no meadow hay at all but only sown hay and clover. Rye grass, red clover, lucerne, sainfoin and white clover were also grown for summer feeding to the horses in the stables, and cut red clover was fed to the cattle.

The value of clover as a winter addition to the hay crop and as a soil-improving agent was soon appreciated by progressive agriculturists. There were problems in adoption however. By 1770 there were still not a great many dykes, hedges or ditch barriers against grazing animals, and stock wandered almost at will during the winter. Thus when John Stewart, a farmer in the Auchterarder area of Perthshire first proposed to sow out red

clover his neighbours were aghast at the prospect of having to
herd and control the movement of their cattle after harvest. This
was an unheard of practice and they petitioned the Sheriff with
a formal complaint against John's innovation—to no avail for
the Sheriff had read the recommendations of the Improvers and
ruled in John's favour. Neighbours had to fence their stock in but
were not obliged to fence other farmers' stock out(35) and an
important new principle was established. As it happened the
following winter was a severe one and John's neighbours were
soon pleading for his hay to save their own stock from starvation.

Flax

Before the general advent of cotton around 1780 the fibre of *linum
usitatissimum*, the cultivated flax, was the main and almost the
only textile fibre available, particularly for sacks and sails but
also for general household use and to a certain extent clothing.
Skins and knitted wool had been utilised in earlier times but the
flax fibre as linen cloth reached its zenith in Scotland in the
eighteenth century. Universally cultivated by almost all those
who worked the land, it was made into thread by men and
women alike as they went around the countryside and in their
homes. As the new-style farms emerged flax offered a good cash
crop, and in Perthshire during the agricultural transition period
most farmers grew some for their own use and some for sale to
others.(31) On the small 6-acre plots of land occupied by
tradesmen about half an acre of flax was grown, to be dressed or
cleaned by the family during the winter evenings.(24) It was
sown later than oats but before the barley crop and conveniently
reaped in July or August before the general harvest. By the latter
quarter of the century 'Strathearn was growing large quantities'.

Harvesting

In the run-rig days and long after, the harvesting of crops was a
hand operation constrained by the nature of the rigs themselves.
Smaller stones were carefully gathered in hazel baskets by the
cottar children and piled out of the way or thrown in the baulks

between the rigs;(20) larger stones were trundled out; those that
could not be so cleared had to be left on the rig to await blasting
by a later generation. In any event the baulks formed effective
divisions every 5 to 9 yards between the lands of the possessors.
Thus these long rigs, longer even than today's fields in some
cases, were readily accessible from both sides for hand
cultivation.

Since the rigs were continuously in grain and without the
cleaning influence of a grass, potato or turnip crop, and since the
individual grain plants were relatively far apart (sowing being
thin) a major and never-ending problem was weeds. During
summer the old men, women and boys pulled the thistles out and
threw them in the baulks where the few horses left at home for the
summer were hand-led periodically to feed on this, almost their
only summer grazing. To facilitate hand-weeding of grain crops
the 'cloutmait'—a wooden tongs—was invented and widely
used to pull out the thistles. The steep ridges of the run-rigs
facilitated access by this peculiar tool whose jaws were 'ten inches
and the handles two foot ten inches and when extended were two
foot asunder'.(20)

Come harvest time grain cropping was purely a hand-sickle
operation, short of pulling out plants by hand or gathering the
grain heads directly. It was near the end of the eighteenth
century before farmers realised that by rolling the ground a
scythe could be used—a more efficient, level-ground technique
which yielded a third more straw than the old rigs. However the
sickle came back into its own to cut flattened grain, so common
with the late harvests of the period, and when, late in the century,
the barley crop was undersown with clover to provide hay. Then
the sickle was used to reap only the heads of the barley and leave
the straw and hay. In the early days shearing was a co-operative
family operation, but when it came to threshing using the flail,
'ilka man swing'it till himsel'.

Once the corn had been cut it was piled in a 12-sheaf parallel
stook—five sheaves on each side of a stook directed to the south-
west to resist the prevailing wind—and covered with two head
sheaves. Workers were often paid by the 'threave', a unit of four
stooks comprising 48 sheaves. On the earlier run-rigs the grain
was tied into very large sheaves as large as two lengths of the
grain would permit, and the binder pressed the cut grain down

with his or her knee and tied it as tightly as possible. However, as wheat came into use the sheaves became so heavy that they could not be moved readily and so the ubiquitous Lord Kames was advocating much smaller sheaves of one length of straw which would be compressed with the arm only. Not only that, but the heavy sheaves took a long time to dry out, being left to stand out for a fortnight, and the noble Lord maintained that with smaller sheaves a week would suffice and the crop could be harvested sooner.

For gathering the crop on the run-rigs two males and one female shared a rig; 'One male and one female share a rope (a band of twisted straw used to bind the sheaves) or one man makes the rope and the two women fill it with corn.' In the former case one person was employed to band the sheaves and set up the stooks on one ridge; in the latter three persons set up stooks for fifteen shearers. On the later farms gangs of workers were organised, doing the same operations but on a broad front. Once the crop was safely home from the rigs threshing was done by the flail, for threshing mills were just starting to come in. A ploughman and his boy would thresh out the day's requirement of straw each morning before yoking time, feeding their team of oxen by candle or lamp light. Comment of the time was that 'this threshing is rather foul and much grain is lost'.(15)

As time went on methods changed. Thus by 1790 stacks were being set up on a pedestal while some farmers were already housing their grain crop indoors in the newly constructed steadings. Also on progressive farms carts and waggons were being used to harvest the grain although on many others the crop was still pulled home on sledges. The long cart, hinged to coup (tip) from the axle, was just coming into use, and this provides an interesting side-light into the economics of the operation. Labour was plentiful and cheap whereas carts were scarce. This caused the load to be couped beside the stack, for rather than delay the cart by doing the forking from it, it was cheaper to fork from the ground in two lifts.(24)

As farms of today's size evolved the universal practice was to engage hands proportionate to the crop, these being days of copious supplies of cheap labour. Part of this supply was the multitude of hand-spinners and weavers, shoemakers, glovers and hand-craftsmen of the day who welcomed a spell in the open

away from the expanding burghs. Thus we read of a Thomas
Wylie of Airlywight, the last of the old farmers to use the heuk
(sickle) in the Perth area, for whom '140 to 160 reapers left
Bankfoot every morning to shear his crop'. Around 1775 weekly
markets for shearers crept in and they became more mobile. As
an example of productivity we read that eighteen female
shearers using sickles took 20 days at 1s. per day to cut the crop
from 110 acres, which worked out at about $3\frac{1}{2}$ days per acre; also
that when bandsters were employed, one to six shearers, to
encourage productivity, each worker got a $\frac{3}{4}$ gill of whisky per
day. Later too 'Lot men' in gangs were employed to work the
flails on the threshing floor. These men were not paid as day
labour but got one twenty-fifth of the grain and their food.(12)

Corn mills and kilns

As has already been stressed, in the run-rig days virtually all the
grain produced was destined for the mouths of those who raised
it, but first it had to be separated from the stalk and then ground.
The first phase, the separation of the grain from the straw, was
universally carried out by the hand labour of the flail until
around 1775. Mostly it was done on the earth floors of the one-
storey barn buildings; winnowing followed, usually inside
between the west-facing open doors of the barn, although it
could be done out of doors on a knoll beside the farm. So long as
the grain was left on the stalk sufficient aeration was caused by
the straw to maintain it in a healthy condition but it was most
important to have it winnowed as quickly as possible after
flailing.(13) The mixture of grain and chaff could spoil very
quickly, especially on the earth floors of the primitive barns. So
long as grain was required only for the farmer's family the whole
operation could be carried out almost daily, but when urban and
country dwellers became segregated and a market developed for
the corn more sophisticated arrangements were essential.

By the last quarter of the century the flail was abandoned and
threshing mills were being constructed at a fast rate. At first these
were operated by hand, then by horse power. Several horses
were yoked to a flat, wheel-like contraption whereby their
endless circling movement was harnessed by gearing in an

enclosed threshing mill within the new steadings. By the nineteenth century these open horse-mills were enclosed by stone walls, their circular open-pillared structure with conical roof and beautifully carpentered rafters becoming an attractive feature of the countryside.

Farms near a source of water soon made use of a water-wheel to power the new machinery and the daily 'thrash' in the darkness of a winter morning would make use of every drop in the newly constructed dams, some having only half an hour's power. Many farmsteads were relocated near this cheap source of power and where several small farming units were combined on enclosure the surviving site was usually the one nearest the stream or else a new one was so located. Long leats were also made to convey water to the farm site. This new pattern with improvements from time to time was to remain relatively static until oil-driven machines took over. True, there was a period when steam-power tried to find a niche in the farming scene, but only a few tall chimneys on water-short locations were built and soon oil was universal.

To dry the grain so that it would keep longer small farm kilns were developed at a very early date, and the old fern touns each had a communal kiln in which each family dried its grain. These kilns were erected on a steep bank in the most exposed and advantageous position within the ferm toun boundaries(31) and were usually fired by peat, as a slow steady heat was essential to dry the damp grain.(12) Sometimes they were even constructed of timber and occasionally they had brick rather than stone floors, an interesting fact since brick was not yet a universal building material and would be foreign in a ferm toun community. Cast iron ribs were eventually used to support the grain as opposed to the wood or stone supports of the early kilns.

In the upper part of the kiln there was an opening or door for the introduction of the grain together with a small observation 'window'. Some of the more advanced kilns had three openings, two on the sides opposite each other, the third opposite the door where the fire was lit.(12) These openings regulated the escape of water-saturated air from the kiln and also controlled the slow burning of the peat fire below. The kiln was very carefully tended by its users, for the wind blowing in the door, which usually faced west, could very easily scorch the grain. As conditions improved the kilns were well built of stone, bonded and made draught-proof with lime mortar—probably the first use of lime mortar by the primitive community. 'They had to be as far as possible fire-proof and were secured from fire by iron beddings or supporters'.(12) To maintain a suitable temperature and aerate the drying grain a pair of bellows was suspended from the door with a long pipe bent up under the fuel, and this blew into the fire periodically to maintain the requisite even temperature.

Following the ferm toun kilns and the hand quern grinding of the family grain came the water-powered mill. It had soon become obvious that to be efficient and economic a mill would have to be large enough to support a full-time miller and his family. Furthermore, competition between mills was eliminated by the thirlage system, devised not so much to protect the miller as to provide him with an income which would afford an adequate rent to the landowner, who put up the initial capital to build the mill.

The *Statistical Account* of 1790 regarding Barry Parish in Angus gives a good account of the Barony mills and the thirlage system. 'The baron built the mill and to finance its structure and to provide a good rent to him from it, a strict system of thirlage was exacted by the baron to the mill.'(33) A fixed proportion of all the grain grown on each individual plot of land had to be handed over to the miller, its value being reflected in due course in the income of the Laird. As in efficient tax structures down the ages every possible source of evasion was closed. The querns had fallen out of use, a process which many landowners had furthered by having the hand querns destroyed so that all grain consumed by the family and its servants had to pass through the estate mills and be liable to toll. 'Even grain that had been fed to the hens had to be accounted for and the thirlage quantity handed over and vassalage paid.'(33) The Barry account is confirmed from Aberdeenshire at the same time. All farms there were thirled to the mill: 'Whether that mill ground their corn or not the grower was bound to pay the miller 1/11 to 1/16 off their crop.'(33) Robertson gives the thirlage in southern Angus as a multure of '5 lippies out of 16 pecks of grain', which amounted to one-thirteenth of the whole. Some mills ground the farmer as well as the grain by insisting on a tenth part! Indeed on the Earl of Fife's estates the multure was stepped up to one-ninth or one-eighth of the crop; in Banffshire, according to Donaldson, the farmers not only paid a mill tax of one-twelfth of their grain but were bound to maintain 'the drains and water-courses thereof in order'; and Anderson of Aberdeenshire complained bitterly of the heavy mill multures and the poor service by the millers.

Spinning and weaving

From being a minor element in the farm economy flax soon became much more important. After the crop was cut or pulled, sheafed in small bundles and stooked like corn, it was normally 'rippled', that is, the stems were drawn by hand through a comblike device to remove the seed. Following that the seed crop was stored in some mouse-proof granary corner and the flax stems sheafed a second time. Then, in the early and mid eighteenth century, the flax fibre, still in the sheaf, was placed in ponds and steeped for four to twelve days, after which it was laid out on short grass to remove the soft matter which had been slackened and made liquid by the steeping. This 'grassing' took around fourteen to twenty-one days. Finally it was dried in an oven, the fibres were broken apart in an engine and scutched and then refined out by passing them through wheels or rollers. At one point Robertson(31) was advocating keeping the lint in stacks till spring to ripen the capsules so as to use more fertile home-produced seed. This however did not find favour with the smaller growers, who wished to complete the rippling and steeping work before the winter months so that the heckling or dressing of the fibres could proceed in the long dark evenings. After all the early operations, which cost 1s.4d.to 1s.6d. per stone, the flax was ready for heckling but its value was now 12s. to 12s.6d. per stone.

As if this were not enough the heckling to make suitable tow for the hand-spinners—machine spinning had still to come— took some time, for the material had to be heckled four times. At this stage the loose open bundles of tow would be placed on the wooden 'rock' or distaff of the spinners, who spun the tow into thread as they went about their day-to-day chores of herding the stock or visiting their friends. The thread they spun was made into balls or cones (spindles) on the wheel, ready for sale to the factory buyers or for hand-weaving at home. In view of all this it is scarcely surprising that the growing of lint as a crop took place largely in the upland glen parishes. James Trotter in the *General View of Agriculture in West Lothian* in 1794 says that flax was never grown to any extent in the Lothians 'chiefly for want of hands, to work it', a remark which stresses the population pressures then existing in the glens and uplands.

In the mid eighteenth century a great deal of the thread for export from country to town was made by the people of Loch Tayside: 'This they do with rocks and spindle as they tend their cattle on the hills.' (28) At this time as many as four fairs each year were held at Kenmore and the Glasgow cloth merchants sent buyers there and also to villages like Letham in Angus to buy hand-spun thread from the run-rig farmers' wives and daughters. At Kenmore as much as £500 changed hands at one fair as the weavers' representatives competed and bargained for this valuable rural commodity; an equal quantity of thread was sold at the Letham fairs. The trade in linen thread built up from 1730 was to endure for two generations before fading with the advent of mechanical spinning.

Between the days of hand-spinning and machine-spinning was the era of the spinning wheel, used at that time more extensively for linen thread than wool production. 'Spinners on the wheel could on average spin two spindles a week at 8*d*. per spindle.' (19) The flax used by this date was chiefly imported, ready dressed, the duty on the importation of raw flax having been removed in 1731. However the demand for home grown flax increased and by 1750 half the flax used in Scotland (apart from Osnaburgs, a coarse imported thread) was home grown. However at this time a subsidy of 15*s*. per acre was being paid to the farmers for flax growing and linen production was a thriving industry. There had been other kinds of encouragement to produce linen, starting with the Act of 1686 which, to encourage the eventual consumption of this hard wearing material, required every person who died to be wrapped and buried in linen under a penalty of £200 Scots for common people and £300 for those in the upper classes. To ensure that the provisions of this Act would be enforced one half of this fine went to the informer and the other half to the poor. In addition the Parish Minister had the onerous task of ensuring that the Act was carried out and in order to prevent evasion he and an elder had to be present at the wrapping and kisting of the body. With cotton virtually unknown till the end of the century home-spun and largely home-woven linen was in universal use. Shirts were made of a coarse sack-like 'harn', and even into the twentieth century remnants of this coarse, hard-wearing linen were still in use by glen women as 'brots' or aprons for coarse work. It was relatively costly due to the cost of the hand-labour involved in making the tow, spinning and weaving. In time however much of the linen spinning was carried out not by rock and spindle but on the spinning wheel, which so quickly superseded the hand-held spindle that soon every family had a wheel, the most costly piece of furniture in the home of that period. However acceptable at home, the wheel was most unpopular in some areas among the women approached to operate them in the first textile factories, which were being promoted by those who saw their money-making potential. John Walker writing to Lord Kames in 1764 from Stornoway tells of the difficulties of starting spinning classes in the Hebrides. The Stornoway lassies would have nothing to do with this new employment. A spinning mistress tried to get a class to use the spinning wheel, and girls as young as twelve were enticed to the class but they ran away as a body and could not be persuaded to join. Considerable pressure was exerted on these young ladies but without avail. Many were obliged to seek early marriage in order to avoid the class! (Married women were not supposed to seek work of this nature.) The class was established eventually and soon women were so quick and expert at this new craft that spinning wheels taking two threads at once were fashioned and a skilful housewife would feed two bundles of linen tow or wool simultaneously into the wheel inlets. Although the two-handed wheels in turn were soon superseded commercially by Arkwright's Spinning Jenny, the old wheels remained, mainly for wool spinning, and for at least 100 years after Arkwright's factories were churning out manufactured thread the glen girls were producing their own hand-spun table cloths and sheets for 'the bottom drawer', sometimes even then from flax grown on their fathers' farms.

In time flax and linen became very important elements in the rural economy. All the farm maid-servants were busy heckling the flax in any spare time they had and there was a demand for buttermilk used by the rapidly expanding bleaching industry. Even wood ashes were in keen demand as a source of alkali for the bleachers, catering for a rising market in quality linen cloth coming for the new machine-spinning linen industry.

The first Scottish linen-spinning machinery was set up at Bervie in 1790 but it was some time before it overcame a peculiar problem. Flax fibre is relatively brittle, a difficulty which the handspinners overcame by continually moistening the tow with saliva but which plagued the machines until 'wet' spinning methods were devised. Incidentally the loss of saliva was thought to be harmful to the spinners but this fear was disregarded as were many of the risks of industry in that era. In any event this human adaptability enabled the host of hand-spinners in the glens to prolong the life of their industry and thus delay somewhat the de-population of the rural areas. Eventually both the processing of flax and the spinning of thread by hand were superseded by machine operations which found their homes in towns and cities. Linen too was displaced by cotton, which in turn had to give ground to man-made fibres.

11 ANIMALS

Sheep

All traces of the early sheep stock of Scotland appear to have been lost through the infusion of other breeds and efforts to improve the quality. Probably the best description of that stock is that by Mr Naismith of Hamilton in the first *Statistical Account* of 1790. He distinguishes between 'those bred in the mountains' and the 'few sheep kept by the farmers' in the lowland areas, the latter being 'of a kind more domestic and refined'. Since he was writing soon after the coming of the black-faced flocks from the borders to supply the midland spinning mills, it could be that we did have a more goat-like breed on the hills as well as a fine-woolled type around the lowland farms. Although the total number of the latter was quite large, individual flocks were small, for the landowners, whose prime motive was then to achieve the maximum number of men on their land, severely restricted the numbers of sheep kept by either the possessors or later the tenant farmers. Sheep were not so mobile as cattle and it was late before a market developed for their wool. They were restricted to such a number per family as would provide clothing for their retainers, and 'were to be eaten on the farm and to provide the clothing for the families' household'.(20) The number of sheep could never exceed the number of cows kept by the individual while that in turn was controlled by the winter feed of the home area. Around four to ten cattle, a similar number of sheep, one to three goats and one horse was the overall ratio of stock grazing which prevented excessive mono-selection of herbage.

The small flocks of three to ten sheep, which 'were carefully selected for beauty and utility', 'were constantly herded and enclosed in a bucht at night with narrow windows and a hurdle door'. 'They were a most improved stock which were killed out when fences were introduced because they ate the new hedges' and 'They cannot now be traced in the country'.(33) Most of these sheep, kept solely to provide wool for the homespun, woven and knitted garments of the run-rig family, had a tough existence. Although almost family pets—'Each child claimed a ewe lamb'—they were often 'starved in summer and almost quite neglected in winter'. 'They are too small, they yield little wool, many of the ewes are barren or miscarry from ill-usage and those that do bring forth lambs have not milk enough to feed them.'(17) They were kept overnight in lean-to shacks against the house walls. 'Those who kept sheep should keep their cots and reives dry and dig in a great quantity of pit earth in the months of June and July for bedding the sheep all winter', whereas 'most of them rot the poor beast with water from above and below and never provide any meat for the stormy time in winter'.(17)

The successive waves of new stock from the south spread quickly, mainly the objective was wool, not mutton. Soon the Cheviot sheep, 'an English breed',(20) were introduced and new forms of sheep farming on a large scale developed. Thus before 1787 General Tom Graham of Balgowan, quick to take advantage of every agricultural innovation, had cleared and enclosed lowland areas to create several 'sheep parks' on his estate near Perth to overwinter the flocks. This rapid expansion of the sheep flocks was due not only to the demand for wool but also to the fact that it was then unthinkable to kill lambs or year-old sheep. The practice was to keep wedder sheep for four to five years before fattening, for the demand for oils and fat throughout the eighteenth century was very high and the production of animal tallow was of prime importance; and the older the sheep the more tallow they could produce. Moreover wool was a steady trade. With wool selling for 9d. a pound, a four year old wedder with a $2\frac{1}{2}$lb fleece could bring in 22s.$\frac{1}{2}d$. per annum, quite apart from the value of the tallow and mutton at the end of its life. The sheep-walk was profitable for owner and tenant and a small sheep farm—which incidentally replaced a ferm toun community of perhaps thirty to forty people and deprived a good many more of their summer pasturage—could in 1790 rent at £140 per annum. The new farmer could count on about £68 profit by breeding sheep or £158 off wedder stock.(31) The capital value of his stock would be around £1,000 and he would employ two shepherds with assistance at shearing time costing about £22.8s.0d. per annum. Thus for those landed proprietors with glens and hills to let there was good profit to be made and by 1790 'much of the yearly income of the gentlemen depended on sheep'.(31) The lands, which brought them little as summer pasturage for their tenants and the multitude of mere possessors who claimed all grazing as an old-established right, were now made available to rent as quickly as the people could be cleared off the ground. Facilitating legislation was produced by the same landowners and used by their lawyers; factors replaced tacksmen; and the clearances were quickly effected and the stage set for a new era.

These developments drastically altered the appearance of the country above the arable line, as a relatively swift change took place from 'a time the hill lands were all grazed by black cattle, hill horses and only partly sheep, to a period in the second half of the century when it was nearly all sheep'(30) and '50,000 sheep grazed the Ochils'.(31) In the early days the pasturage in the border hills and northern valleys was rich and the growing sheep flocks 'were herded from dawn to dusk and guided from one pasturage to the other'.(20) Soon the mountains were harnessed to sheep culture and their whole appearance changed. Under the impact of ranch-type husbandry grazing by sheep all year, instead of cattle and horses in summer, soon eliminated the more nourishing grasses, and reduced upland Scotland, which up till then had an abundant alpine floral covering, to a watery desert populated by the few plants that could survive. All natural regeneration of trees was inhibited. Furthermore with the coming of the large flocks the old practice of muir-burning became universal, which of course 'considerably altered the appearance of the heaths and mountains'.(20) In the absence of estate march-dykes and fences the 'black facers' had all the mountains and most of the valleys to roam on, and the new breed of border shepherds who had followed the flocks north had to contain them as best they could. The change in the landscape is difficult for us to visualise today but Osgood Mackenzie as late as 1850, still could see, in one isolated glen near his home at Loch Ewe, what Scotland had been like before the advent of universal sheep farming. This glen had never been grazed by sheep, only

by cows and cattle. 'As a consequence there was a perfect jungle of primroses, bluebells and honeysuckle and all sorts of orchids, including the fragrant orchid and the now extinct helleborine. The orchids had formerly whitened the ground.'(27)
Large-scale production of wool naturally led to new developments in its use quite apart from export. Thus hand-spinning, wheel-spinning, weaving and knitting first by hand then by machine, were practised in different places, at different times and in different ways. First they were individual activities undertaken mainly by rural women, but as machines were invented and set up in the towns the jobs and the women moved with them. Similarly the small possessor became redundant, deprived of his livelihood by the elimination of his ancient right to graze and fatten his little flock on the mountain parts of his parish or clan lands.

Horses and carts

In the eighteenth century relatively large numbers of horses were maintained. Long before their use for haulage and ploughing they were required as the only transport of people and goods, while on the run-rig holdings they were used almost equally with oxen for ploughing and general haulage. In these early days there was little work for a horse in the summer months, but as roads were made carts could be used and trade in farm goods developed. More and more horses were required and these had to be maintained from the farm produce. 'In the areas where oxen were still exclusively kept to a ripe age for ploughing, horses were still required to drive dung and to take corn to the market.'(15) Both had dual uses, the ox also being used as a source of suet, the horse as the only form of personal transport.
The use of horses and oxen varied most curiously in different areas: horses were used exclusively in Loch Tayside for ploughing(11) but were not used for that purpose north of the Highland Line nor in the west; the Laird of Breadalbane used oxen to plough the home farm lands but not so his tenants nearby.(11) Horses were also required for harrowing, an operation unsuitable for draught oxen, which were used mainly in the spring months for ploughing. Thus by the time larger

farms had developed some farmers found it necessary to keep ten
to twelve oxen for ploughing and six horses for harrowing and
carriages.(15) Reasons for the continued use of oxen for
ploughing were not only the need for massive yet tractable
motive power for the Scots plough (still required for relatively
untilled land) but also the relatively slow development of a
suitable type of horse. The tendency was to breed much lighter
horses than would have been the case had their main purpose
been as draught animals.(11) The first of the large plough horses
which evolved is mentioned in the *General View of Agriculture in
West Lothian*, for in that area more attention had been paid to the
breeding of good stallions. The relatively slow development of
the horse as a draught animal however was due mainly to poor
feeding and care.

Like other farm animals, horses had an extremely hard life.
When the spring labour was finished in May, the cattle and some
horses were sent off to the summer pasture as much as 10 to 30
miles away, and there they lived on the hill shielings until the end
of August. Those horses which were not sent to the hills had to be
carefully tended on the cultivated farm lands for there were no
fences apart from the hill dykes between the outbye land and the
moor, and horses had to be tethered at all times. During the day
they would be led on a halter along the baulks and there they
would graze on the native weeds and thistles as well as those
removed by hand from the rigs. Part of the pasture land was
reserved for horse grazing and was known as 'hained grass', the
remainder being reserved for hay or cut for the family cow. Those
kept on the home ground could only pick up what little grazing
was available in competition with the few milch cattle of the ferm
toun, and when the cattle came home from the hills in autumn
the horses had even more competition. As far as feed was
concerned, in 1763 four stones of bruised whins was reckoned to
be adequate. Even as late as 1813 Headrick of Dunnichen was
commenting on the fact that horses were still fed in summer
largely on thistles which 'were removed from the growing corn
with long wooden forceps' but 'were esteemed since they were
the only summer feed available'.(18) Thus 'It was a good farmer
who could boast in spring that none of his horses or oxen had
fainted with fatigue from spring labour.'(12) The introduction
of clover as a crop was the answer to all this under-nourishment

and as time went on the better farmers had stables erected for the horses, and 'there they were fed on cut grass all summer together with the new crops of green ryegrass, red clover, sainfoin, lucerne and white clover'.(24) On the old ferm toun lands however 'there was no enclosure in the hands of a tenant that could hold a horse if it could see corn'.(24)

Part of the story of the horse is the story of the cart, which evolved as an agricultural vehicle in Scotland only in the eighteenth century. For the first half of that period there were virtually no wheeled vehicles on the run-rig farms (Figure 8). Nor was there much need for them since the holdings were extremely small and had no end product that could not 'walk' to market, and in any case there were no roads apart from massively rutted tracks between the larger towns. Furthermore the nature of the rigs and baulks made wheeled movement either across or along them virtually impossible. Instead 'bulky loads were carried by currans' ('a hurdle fixed to each side of a horse by means of a hooked saddle') while smaller articles were carried in hinged hampers.(30) Crops could be brought in by sledge but this required a track or road of sorts whereas all sorts of materials—crops, dung, peat, coal for example—could be carried by curran without such constraint. The transport of peat or divot was a much bigger problem than the short journeys of the harvest gathering and as peat sources were exhausted long tracks were cut into the hillsides by heavily laden horses.

Not only horses but humans also were used as beasts of burden to carry creels or baskets, and Pennant in 1769 paints a shocking picture of conditions on the larger home farms of that period and especially the heavy burdens placed on women: 'Females are the only animals of burden. They turn their backs to the dunghills and receive in their "keises" or baskets, as much as is flung in with pitch forks and then trudge to the fields in droves of sixty or seventy.'(28)

The introduction of the cart to rural areas was sporadic. The first use of carts in rural Aberdeenshire took place in 1765, while further north in Invernesshire 'no iron shod wheel had entered the Parish of Cawdor in Inverness and Nairn up to 1790'.(33) This reference to 'iron shod' does not preclude possible earlier use of cruder, unshod carts. Farther north still Mackenzie claimed that in the Poolewe area carts were not used until 1848:

8   The first of the carts.

'Up to then everything was carried on horseback or by
sledge.'(27) Nevertheless in Angus the old single-horse carts
were rapidly going out of use by 1790: 'Two horse carts are now
a prestige symbol.'
The first carts were very crude. Robertson confirms that the
early carts in the Callander area 'had wheels which were fixed to
the axle; no spokes or naves, just solid planks in three sections like
the bottom of a cart,' while relics from the Angus glens show
wooden axles of hazel and pine with pin holes for centring
wooden wheels. These early carts were primitive 'small single-
horse carts, made of home wood without the bark being taken
off'; small—'not much bigger than a wheelbarrow'; and heavy—
'They weigh about 7½ cwt.'(14) By 1790 further progress is
reported: 'Iron axles are coming into general use.'(16)

Cattle

The cattle of the old possessors—the 'kyloes'—were generally
black, relatively small and hardy enough to lie out all winter
under the most severe conditions, which is what they and the
horses had to do. The milch cow and possibly a follower lived
with the farmer's family in their crude house while the sheep
were enclosed in a lean-to at the gable end, safe from fox and
wolf.
During their early years these cattle had a hard life. In the
uplands and glens so many stock were raised that winter survival
was problematic: 'The black cattle could only produce a calf
every second year through sheer starvation' and 'Calves born
before the first of March had little chance of survival'. As far as
winter fodder on the farms was concerned 'from Candlemas to
Spring all the cattle were in desperate straits for food and many
died. A third, a half, or even a greater number could perish on
each farm, from sheer lack of food'(20), there being no turnips,
potatoes or sown hay at that time. As four-year-olds they would
be brought down to central Perthshire or the borders where they
would be fattened on the better pasture before moving via the old
drove roads to England, heavy with tallow for southern candles
which would light the homes, churches and the early candle-lit
spinning and weaving mills.

As for the lowland 'knouts', writing of the possessors on the Stobhall Estate in Lowland Perthshire Wight says 'they kept too many cattle. The fodder in the winter is all used up and the beasts even starved'; 'All the yeld cattle are sent to the Highlands in the summer for want of grass. The whole set up is poor, barren, half starved and poverty stricken.'(35) Thus in the parishes which had no detached portion for summer grazing, the farmers, raising too many stock for their own ground, had to depend on the summer grazing of the uplands for their stock so as to preserve their own limited ground for winter use. Another difficulty was the lack of winter herding: 'There was no restraint whatsoever on the movement of cattle in the winter time. The herds wandered anywhere. They were herded only in the summer time.'(20) Eventually 'grown on for six years during which time they put on a little fat or tallow .... in the seventh year they were better fed and fattened up for the butcher'(20), by which time the owner had had three years' work out of them as draught oxen.

As time went on farmers in some areas were selecting their stock with some care and distinctive Scottish types were evolving. 'The Buchan breed is being vastly improved by selection and better feeding with some turnips, as to be 20 to 30 stones when fat'(13) and though they had no distinctive name as yet the origins of the Aberdeen Angus breed were being established. In addition as the housing of animals in courts and shelters grew and as byres for stall-fed beasts became the rule in the new steadings, greater care began to be taken of the animals. Plentiful cheap labour was available and little heed was taken of the cost of men's time. Thus Lord Kames in 1780 advised that feeding cattle, by then carefully housed in byre stalls in the new large farms, should be brushed daily and washed once a week! The cattle were still bled once a month—for their health rather than for the owner's food as in earlier times. Veal calves, also bled regularly, were housed in the dark from birth until ready for the butcher.(24) With the larger farms and stone-built shelters it was possible to over-winter a mature beast to make a cash profit of 10s. per head, and this was apart from the valuable manure from the open courts. Towards the end of the century turnips were grown and fed to cattle in byre stalls, and distillers utilising the spent malt draff were also fattening off a lot of cattle in byres near the distilleries, 'and in a very good season could undersell the farmers to the town butchers'.(31) In this way the three distilleries in Kincardine fattened 320 oxen each winter and spring. There were technical advances too: 'In some cases the byre is floored in rafters ½ inch apart with a pit below to catch the urine and dung.'(31) This was a reflection not only of a practice which staged a comeback 150 years later, but also on the availability—so soon after its extreme scarcity at the beginning of the century—of timber for the cattle flooring 'rafters'.

By 1785 cattle were used only for meat and milk production, being maintained as draught oxen only by a few lairds who kept teams for cultivation of the home farms (11) and more as a status symbol than for their practical worth. While heavy horses were sought by the new farmers as draught animals the Laird's horses, his pride and joy, were for hunting and carriage purposes. But his cattle also came to be pampered in the massive new home-farm steadings, being lavishly kept in byres and fed with the new crop of red clover, cut and carried in regularly by the cattlemen. In fact some went so far as to have a bed made up for the stockman in the byre buildings so that he could 'attend to them during the night'.(24) Apart from such extravagances however, the enclosure of the land into separate fields was generally a good thing for cattle and a far cry from the days when the herd lassies and their cattle were chased by dogs whenever they trespassed onto their neighbour's ground.

In the first half of the century 'there was nothing but salt meat all winter'.(24) Towards the end however improvements in agriculture, chiefly in grazing, meant that 'it was possible to get fresh meat all the year round although it was dearer in spring'.(24) Salt meat was not only for home consumption but also for export, and in particular the grazier's supply of salt meat to the navy became important. Unfortunately there was a heavy duty on the production of salt at that time, so that Irish farmers, who could buy salt at a much lower duty, were sometimes able to monopolise this lucrative trade. The price of salt was a sore complaint of the Aberdeenshire farmers.(13)

As time went on and the towns and villages grew, a trade developed in milk, which had hitherto been the responsibility of each individual family. Estates, which needed to keep the castle and its retainers adequately supplied, could maintain cow byres and a dairymaid for their exclusive use, just as the earlier monasteries had done. Thus although milk was still considered a seasonal trade—since cows had meagre provisions all winter—there were growing markets for it and for butter and cheese, especially in cities like Glasgow. In addition dairying was becoming popular with the new gentlemen farmers, who no longer needed martial status to impress their rivals. With these incentives much more attention was given to breeding and some of the classic breeds, such as Ayrshires, began to be developed. As the rigs were levelled on the farms, however, the old black 'kyloe' was fast disappearing.

Poultry

Nothing illustrates the contrast between the affluence of our day and the subsistence level of living in the eighteenth century better than poultry. Virtually all the edible parts of oats and barley were sorely needed by the people for their own use, and because of the complete lack of surplus food grains very few poultry could be kept by the run-rig farmers. A few 'kain' fowl lived in the rafters of the turf hovels, and geese could pick up a living on the odd blade of grass escaping the grazing animals but both of these animals counted as rent. And during the summer months a few chickens that had foraged outside for themselves might be had as a delicacy. But the keeping of hens on the farms and by the retainers on the estates was discouraged. In the latter case the fear that the Laird's corn might be fed to the employees' hens was enough to bring a ban on fowls near the home farm; on the farms the jealous miller and the Laird saw to it that where hens were kept strict account was kept of their grain consumption so that the mill thirlage quantity could be closely calculated and vassalage strictly paid. In our day and in theirs 'chicken feed' had entirely different meanings!

Pigs

In the run-rig days there were few pigs. As in the case of poultry this was due in the first place to the absence of food for this scavenging type of animal; there were no deciduous forests in

Scotland for them to roam in; and while a few oak woods existed in rocky gorges and on the west coast the acorn harvests were few and far between. On the ferm toun there was virtually no waste; any grain surplus to the food needs of the inhabitants was carefully treasured for the whisky stills; while the waste from the still in turn was too erratic to be relied on and too dangerous to be seen in public! Later the new tenant farmers began to raise pigs since they had the food for them, but so long as the small ferm toun families lived off their strips of land pigs were entirely out of the question.

A second factor was that the Highlanders, like the Jew, abhorred animals which did not chew the cud; in 1765 'swine were proscribed on the whole of the Breadalbane land'.(19) Furthermore as the displaced families started a new life in the towns they carried this dislike with them: 'A few swine were kept by several farmers but the bulk of the people are not fond of their flesh.'(16) Thus although 'by the latter end of the century swine were raised in considerable numbers at all the mills and distilleries in Banffshire and a few by the principal tenant farmers'(15) there was so little demand for them by the local populace that an outside market had to be sought. This was found in an export trade from Aberdeen, where the butchers would buy up herds of two or three hundred pigs at a time from the distilleries for processing and shipping to southern markets.

With the introduction of potatoes the whole scene changed, for every household soon kept a pig to use up the abundant waste from the new crop. By this time the rural populace was much reduced and the land workers still being displaced from the enclosed farms often existed for a time in 'model' villages built for them by rural estates. Among the ruins of these rows of rural cottages can be seen even larger rows of stone-built pig sties, which supported a life on pork and potatoes for a generation before these inhabitants too drifted away. These ghost villages can still be traced in some of the Perthshire glens, and the rows of pig sties seem oddly out of place in areas where, a generation before they were built, pig meat was looked on with horror and even banished by the Laird's decree.

Wild animals

In the hungry run-rig days anything edible was hunted by everyone employing all the means available. But these means were limited by the absence of efficient 'fowling pieces' and limited ownership of firearms generally—quite apart from their proscription in the Highlands. Thus large numbers of predators must have survived which reduced the numbers of birds and animals available to man. Wolves, the natural control of red deer, were virtually extinct by the eighteenth century, although they had been a menace to the farmer not so long before. Nevertheless man and dogs had reduced the numbers of deer, numbers which were very low compared with those now surviving on the Highland's managed deer forests. Don of Forfar who probably knew the Caenlochan and Balmoral deer forests better than any man before or since, reported only a very few deer in the huge mountain areas he botanised. His comment in 1800 was 'only a rare stag', while Headrick the Angus botanist confirms their lack of numbers in 1813: 'Deer (are) now banished from our Grampians' and 'Only a few stragglers come down'.(18) Similarly there were few grouse: heather-burning was not then an organised activity and there were many more eagles and hawks to prey upon them. In the lower lands rabbits were moving into Scotland late in the century encouraged by the early gamekeepers, who constructed warrens for their propagation. Trout, in the period before rod-and-line river fishing or otter trawling on the fresh water lochs, were very plentiful. Rods and even suitable hooks were not available for general use, although some use could be made of the nets customarily used for salmon. Salmon also were plentiful and were netted to great effect on all the rivers, and 'leisters',—three pronged spears—were extensively used as a legitimate weapon. Around 1785 estuary netting was extended to the sea beaches, and off suitable headlands fixed and bowed nets were found to be so very effective that the huge numbers early available were eventually reduced. But it took some time to perfect this new style of netting and Anderson claims that in his time 'the numbers so caught were inconsiderable'.(13) The salmon were pickled with salt and vinegar and sent in casks by sea to London, Paris and the Mediterranean ports of Genoa and Leghorn. The practice of building large ice houses let into the hillside near netting stations meant that iced boxes of fresh salmon, and lobster too, could also be sent. The ice was taken from local ponds and stored with sawdust in the ice houses.

Not all wild animals were benign of course and perhaps at least as much energy had to be spent on protecting man's interests against predators. Thus towards the end of the century as sheep replaced cattle on the hill pastures fox hunters were in keen demand by farmers. By 1775 these hunters were already organised into regular districts and were paid a fixed sum by the farmers and landowners of these areas.(30) Robertson advocated that instead they be paid for each fox killed, a procedure that had been successfully applied to the extermination of the wolf. The sum was gradually increased as foxes grew scarcer, and by the latter half of the century it was no longer necessary for sheep to be housed indoors overnight. Then at one time during the change from run-rig farming to cash cropping, moles were proving a nuisance. 'There was no way yet of killing them apart from digging them out' says Lord Kames and this was carried out as part of the farming routine between 'The first of May old style and the first of May new style'.

All too typically the estate owners claimed exclusive rights to all wild fowl and animals, and from 1632 no man was allowed to shoot deer, blackcocks, etc without the laird's licence under pain of £20.(36) In a further effort to eliminate poaching the Earl of Breadalbane laid down that no one could harbour poachers in any way, 'to give them meat, drink, house room or any kind of beild'; all had to co-operate in vermin killing.

REFERENCES

1 Andrew Fletcher of Saltoun (1784)

2 Andrew Lang

3 W J Watson, *Foreword to A Stewart's Highland Parish*

4 *Balgowan Papers* (Register House)

5 Plan Broomlands etc 1769 (*Balgowan Papers*) Duncan McLeish

6 Rev Donald Sage, *Memorablia Domestica* writing in 1889 of 1715

7 Rev R Edward, *County of Angus 1678* (translated from Latin of Robert Edward)

8 *An economic history of the Hebrides and Islands of Scotland* (University, 1760–86)

9 E E Gauldie, *Scottish Bleachfields* (University Library, Dundee)

10 Mr Fullerton of Gallerie writing to Mr Hope of Rankeillour, 1750

11 Farquharson and McArthur, *Survey of Loch Tayside* (1769)

12 Rev Mr Rodger, *General View of the Agriculture of Forfar and Angus* (1794)

13 Dr James Anderson, *General View of the County of Aberdeen* (1794)

14 John Francis Erskine, *General View of the Agriculture of the County of Clackmannan* (1795)

15 Jas Donaldson, *General View of the County of Banff* (1794)

16 James Trotter, *General View of the Agriculture of West Lothian* (1794)

17 *Gordons Mill Farming Club. 1758-1764* (Aberdeen University Studies)

18 Rev J Headrick of Dunnicham (1853)

19 *Interests of Scotland considered* (1733)

20 John Walker DD Professor of Natural History Edinburgh (1764 writing to Lord Kames) *An economic History of the Highlands and Islands 1760-1786*

21 J M Davidson, *Proceedings of the Scottish Anthropological and Folklore Society 1948*

22 James Anderson LLD, *Essays relating to Agriculture and Rural Affairs* (1764)

23 Sir John Sinclair of Ulbster

24 Lord Hendry Home Kames 1760–80. Several books including *Gentleman Farmer* (1766)

25 Rev Mason Inglis, *Annals of Auchterhouse*

26 H Adamson, *Muses of Trednodle* (1638)

27 Osgood Mackenzie, *Relics of an every day life* (1850)

28 Thomas Pennant, *Tour of Scotland. 1769*

29 Provost Patrick Lindsay (1733)

30 Rev J Robertson, Callander, *A General View of Agriculture, etc. 1799*

31 —— *General View in the Southern Areas of Perth 1794*

32 Robert Heron, *General view of the Natural Circumstances of the Hebrides. 1780-1790*

33 *Statistical Account 1790*

34 *The Treatise of Agriculture 1762*

35 *Wights' Husbandry 1773*

36 Wm A Gilles, *In Famed Breadalbane. 1938*

37 W J Watson, *A Stewart's Highland Parish*

38 Rev J Headrick of Dunnichen (1813)

GLOSSARY

Bere	A primitive form of barley
Birleyman	This was a prominent resident who usually acted as arbiter or spokesman for his members of the ferm toun or community; Or a member of the Birlie-court The Birlie-court was a court of country neighbours to settle local concerns, etc.
Branks	A bridle for scolds, witches, etc; Or a bridle or halter for horses or cows when at grass or tethered
Bridewells	Houses of correction
Bross	Oatmeal or peasemeal mixed with boiling water or milk
Chas-chrom	Hand dug by a primitive tool
Cleek	A salmon gaff or fishing net, or a hook for a kettle
Cottar	A co-terminous dweller, dependent on local work on a neighbouring farm
Creepie	A low stool or a milking stool
Croft	Land of superior quality, kept constantly manured and under crop
Cruik	The cruik trusses of the rural cottages were placed about six feet apart and they supported horizontal branches carrying the thatch. They were formed of short tree limbs dowelled together and sprang from near floor level. These were used instead of rafters owing to the scarcity of suitable wood
Draff	Grain husks or spent grain
Excambion	An exchange of land
Feal	This fuel was the uncultivated grass root top soil, entirely vegetative and centuries old
Feus	Land held in perpetuity, or for 99 years, generally in payment of a yearly rent
Gadsman	This was the name given to the person carrying a pointed stick to prod the horses
Girnal	A meal chest or store

Greeting bairns	Crying children
Heckle	To cross-question a candidate for honours at a public meeting; to examine searchingly
Herd	A farm-servant who tends cattle; or the coarse refuse of flax
Inbye	The 'inbye' or 'infield' land was the ground nearest the dwellings which was continuously cultivated as arable land
Jougs	A form of pillory fixed round offenders necks
Kale	Colewort or cabbage, also vegetable soup
Keis	A large straw basket for carrying on a person's back
Kisting	The act of placing a dead body in a coffin
Knout	Cattle
Kyloe	A breed of small Highland cattle
Leat	A dugout lade or made water channel
Mells	A large wooden hammer, or mallet
Memorial	A written representation of facts
Merk	A silver coin, worth $13\frac{1}{2}$ sterling
Mosses	Places where peat may be dug
Mulct	Fines held in Church funds and used for special purposes
Multure	The toll of meal taken by a miller for grinding grain
Otter	A wooden device for dragging a fishing line over a loch
Outbye	The 'outbye' or 'outfield' land was further from the dwellings and only occasionally cultivated
Pendicle	A pendicle was a very small farm or croft, sometimes attached to a larger unit
Pendicler	A pendicler was an inferior tenant
Quern	A stone hand mill to crush grain
Rieve	To plunder
Riske	Wet boggy land
Rock	The wooden staff that carried the unwoven flax or wool
Scutched	A combing device used in flax dressing
Spindle	The stone or metal rotated to form thread
Steading	Buildings distinguished from the farmhouse, sheltering farm work and animals
Spit	The depth of a spade in digging
Stickit	Unsuccessful or failing
Stock	Farm animals
Stook	A number of sheaves of grain
Tack	A lease holding a farm, between the landowner and the farmer

Tacksman	A leaseholder, between the landowner and the tenant
Thirlage	Servitage to a particular mill
Thirled	To bind a tenant by lease to grind his grain at a certain mill; compelled to use
Thole	Tolerate, suffer
Tithes	Percentage of land products allotted to parish minister
Toft	A bed for plants of cabbage, etc, or land once tilled but now abandoned
Yeld	A barren cow or ewe, ceasing to give milk